HARVARD SEMITIC MONOGRAPHS

Volume I

For Mrs. Pal S. Ellenbogen
all Best Wishes

James Donald Shenkel

Chronology
and
Recensional Development
in the Greek Text of Kings

JAMES DONALD SHENKEL

Harvard University Press
Cambridge, Massachusetts
1968

Distributed in Great Britain by Oxford University Press, London

Library of Congress Catalog Card Number 68–21983

Printed in the United States of America

PREFACE

The present study is a revised version of my doctoral dissertation by the same title, which was submitted to Harvard University in September 1964. In reworking the dissertation I have incorporated further research and have brought the bibliography up to date.

I wish to take this opportunity to express my gratitude to Professor Frank Cross of Harvard University. It was he who first directed my attention to the significance of the Qumran discoveries for an understanding of the historical development of the Greek and Hebrew texts in the Old Testament. As director of my dissertation Professor Cross was an unfailing source of advice and encouragement and later was instrumental in having this study accepted for publication in the Harvard Semitic Monographs series.

I would also like to thank Professor Patrick W. Skehan of the Catholic University of America for his critical reading of the manuscript and the helpful suggestions he has made.

J.D.S.

Woodstock College
November 1967

CONTENTS

ABBREVIATIONS

A	Codex Alexandrinus
B	Codex Vaticanus
BASOR	*Bulletin of the American Schools of Oriental Research*
DA	Dominique Barthélemy, *Les Devanciers d'Aquila* (Leiden, 1963)
HTR	*Harvard Theological Review*
JAOS	*Journal of the American Oriental Society*
JBL	*Journal of Biblical Literature*
KR	The Καίγε Recension
L	The Lucianic text
LXX	The Septuagint
MT	Masoretic text
OT	Old Testament
RB	*Revue Biblique*
VT	*Vetus Testamentum*
ZAW	*Zeitschrift für die alttestamentliche Wissenschaft*
ZNW	*Zeitschrift für die neutestamentliche Wissenschaft*

INTRODUCTION

One of the most important results of the discovery of biblical manuscripts in the Judean wilderness some twenty years ago has been the revival of interest in the study of the Greek text of the Old Testament.[1] It was only to be expected that manuscripts found in the caves at Qumran would reflect a text type closely resembling the Masoretic text (MT). The surprising discovery was the manuscripts displaying a Hebrew text type with readings similar to those found in Greek biblical texts.[2] The existence of such Hebrew manuscripts proves conclusively that various text types of the Hebrew Bible existed side by side before the adoption by Palestinian rabbis at the turn of the first century of the Common Era of the consonantal text underlying the MT. As this latter text acquired normative status, divergent Hebrew text types ceased to be copied. Because the Old Greek translation had been based upon one of these divergent types, Jewish scholars prepared new recensions with the intention of making the Greek translation correspond more closely to the MT.

However, the Greek Bible had long since become the property of the Christian Church as well as of Judaism. Recognition on the part of Palestinian rabbis of the normative character of the MT did not immediately result in the disappearance of divergent textual traditions among the Greek biblical manuscripts. Only with the text-critical labors of Origen did the tendency then prevalent in Judaism of equating the MT with the *hebraica veritas* gain entrance into the Church. This same conviction was subsequently to motivate Jerome's translation of the Hebrew Bible into Latin. But the growing popularity of versions based upon the MT never succeeded entirely in eliminating ancient textual traditions from the Bible of the Church. This conservatism, especially of the Eastern Church, was due in large part to the sacred character that the ancient Greek version, traditionally designated as the Septuagint, had acquired among the Church Fathers before the ascendancy of the MT.[3]

Remnants of ancient textual traditions were thus preserved until modern times in the biblical manuscripts in Greek, and in other versions based upon them, although the proper historical perspective for an understanding of these variant traditions had been lost. The late nineteenth century witnessed a revival of Septuagint scholarship with the ambitious program of Paul de Lagarde for reconstructing the proto-Septuagint by assigning the various extant Greek manuscripts to one or another of the three principal recensions described by Jerome: the Origenic, the Lucianic, and the Hesychian.[4] The most substantial result of this endeavor has been the identification of the Lucianic recension in certain OT books.[5]

Diametrically opposed to the line of research initiated by Lagarde was the theory of Paul Kahle that the Septuagint did not stand at the beginning of the development of the Greek textual tradition but was rather the end product of a process of selective canonization of local translations or "targums."[6] Other scholars, especially Gehman and Wevers, although adhering to the basic principles of Lagarde, have attempted to explain the divergences of the Greek text from the MT as due to translation idiosyncrasies and editorial reworking of the ancient text in the interests of theology or other tendentious ends.[7] The recent textual discoveries in the Judean desert have vindicated the essential soundness of the Lagardian position, as opposed to that of Kahle,[8] and have called into question the theories of the Gehman school as they have been applied to the historical books of the OT.[9]

The discovery of the biblical scrolls in the Judean desert has provided actual manuscript evidence for the historical evolution of the Hebrew text before the stabilization of the Masoretic consonantal text. In addition, this evidence will also permit the reconstruction of the parallel development of the Greek text, which was continually revised toward the evolving Hebrew text. The official publication of the new manuscript evidence is still in the preliminary stages. Nevertheless, sufficient material has already been made available to allow the first attempts at scientific and controlled reconstruction of the development of the Greek and Hebrew texts.[10]

The Books of Samuel have been the subject of the most important discussions to date because the richest manuscript evidence for an early Hebrew text has been found for them. Frank M. Cross, Jr., entrusted with the official publication of the several Samuel manuscripts from Cave IV at Qumran, has already produced two articles on this material[11] and has undertaken the reconstruction of the history of the development of the biblical text in three further studies, largely on the basis of his research in the Books of Samuel.[12] Dominique Barthélemy, responsible for the publication of the Greek Minor Prophets scroll, has advanced a comprehensive theory of the development of the Greek text. The principal subject of the textual analyses upon which his hypothesis of a new Greek recension rests is the Second Book of Samuel.[13]

Little has been discovered by way of direct manuscript evidence from Qumran for the Books of Kings.[14] However, the Greek text found in the majority of extant manuscripts, including the most important uncial, the Codex Vaticanus (B), has the same character throughout the Books of Samuel and Kings, as will be shown in the following chapter. The type of study, then, that Cross and Barthélemy have already undertaken for the text of Samuel can also be extended profitably to the Books of Kings, as Barthélemy has suggested.[15] The methodological principles developed on the basis of the recent manuscript discoveries are valid for all four Books of Samuel and Kings or, as they are called perhaps more appositely in Greek, the four Books of Reigns.[16]

With respect to content, the Books of Kings offer a unique advantage for research into the variant readings of the Greek text because of the chronological data they contain. It is apparent upon even casual inspection that the Greek and Hebrew texts of Kings contain conflicting chronological data. This divergence not only involves at times a difference of number in the synchronisms for the regnal years but also entails major transpositions in the order of the text. These transpositions have been made necessary by the disparate data, and in turn they give rise to the creation of doublets in the text, which can be explained satisfactorily only in the light of the recensional development of the Greek text.

In the history of biblical scholarship innumerable attempts have been made to comprehend the chronological data in the Books of

Kings and to reconstruct a coherent chronology. But only those studies that have given serious attention to the data of the Greek texts can pretend to be adequate. Moreover, it is necessary to investigate the methodological presuppositions of even those scholars who devote considerable space to the discussion of the evidence from the Greek texts. Two comparatively recent and widely influential monographs on the chronology in Kings may serve to illustrate this observation.

Joachim Begrich prefers the theoretical position of Kahle to that of Lagarde with respect to Septuagint origins.[17] As a consequence, though Begrich reconstructs his chronology in part on the basis of variant readings taken from the mass of Greek manuscripts, he does so without regard for the recensional history of the Greek text.[18]

Edwin R. Thiele, in the first edition of his book on the chronological data in Kings, has a lengthy chapter on the variant figures of the Greek text.[19] These data of the Greek text, however, never enter into the reconstruction of the biblical chronology, which he bases exclusively on the data of the MT, for which he has an extremely conservative esteem. In his treatment of the Greek data Thiele betrays little awareness of the historical evolution of the Greek and Hebrew texts. For him the Greek variant readings are but late and inaccurate modifications of the earlier and more correct data of the MT.[20]

In the revised version of his book,[21] Thiele has simply omitted the chapter on the chronological data of the Greek texts. As a substitute, a few paragraphs in the concluding chapter of the book[22] are devoted to the Greek data. But he does now admit that the variant Greek data could already have been present in the Hebrew *Vorlage* of the original Greek translators.[23]

The present study is not concerned with the elaboration of a new chronology but with the reexamination of the Greek text of Kings, one of the primary sources for any adequate reconstruction of a chronology. The basic importance of this type of source criticism was pointed out over fifty years ago by A. T. Olmstead, who made many valuable observations on the development of the text of Kings.[24] It is hoped that a better understanding of the recensional development of the Greek text will provide a new perspective for conducting research into the chronology of the Books of Kings.

Recensional Development in the Greek Text of Samuel and Kings

Any treatment of the chronological problems in the Books of Kings would be inadequate unless it were based upon an understanding of the Greek text as an independent body of traditions deserving of study in its own right, and not merely as a source for occasionally interesting variants to readings found in the Masoretic text.[1] The purpose of this chapter is to provide such an understanding by distinguishing the successive phases in the evolution of the Greek text and indicating their relationship to the parallel development of the Hebrew text.

In chronological sequence the major stages in the history of the Greek text were: 1. the Old Greek;[2] 2. proto-Lucian;[3] 3. the καίγε recension;[4] and 4. the recension of Origen known as the Hexapla.[5] These four are important because of their Hebrew *Vorlagen*. The first three of these Greek text forms correspond to the principal local types of the pre-Masoretic Hebrew text. The last mentioned Greek recension represents the most influential assimilation of the Greek text to the MT.[6]

The classic approach of the Lagardian school to Septuagint research is adopted in the present study as a working hypothesis. There was one original translation of a Hebrew text of Samuel and Kings into Greek.[7] Its relationship to the translation into Greek of the Pentateuch and the other OT books is not yet clear. Much work remains to be done on Septuagint origins. Each book, or closely related set of books, must be studied separately. What is said here concerning the Books of Samuel and Kings would have to be verified in every case before being considered applicable to the other books of the Greek Bible. All versions of the Greek text of Samuel and Kings subsequent to the Old Greek translation were recensions of the Old Greek and not new translations.[8]

The use of the term "recension" here is analogical. Perhaps "text form" would be a more suitable designation. The three principal revisions under discussion have this in common: that they were based upon the Old Greek and represented corrections toward a developing Hebrew text. The manner and extent of the revision, however, varies in each case. Proto-Lucian differs from the Old Greek in a number of readings, but in general has the same order and structuring. The KR differs widely from the two earlier text forms in both its structure and the characteristic way in which it renders certain Hebrew expressions. Origen's revision of the Greek text toward conformity with the MT was not a direct reworking of the earlier Greek text itself, but an assimilation made with the help of the late Greek versions.

Each of the major recensions involved a correction toward a Hebrew text that differed from the one underlying the previous stage of the Greek text. It was precisely the development of the Hebrew text, considered as the standard of textual probity, that prompted the successive revisions of the Greek text. The two earliest recensions, proto-Lucian and the KR, were the products of Jewish scholarship, whereas the hexaplaric recension resulted from Origen's recognition of the normative value of the text used by the rabbis in his day. There were other reasons, of course, for undertaking the new revisions. One such motivation was the desire to have a uniform rendition of certain Hebrew expressions into Greek. This translation practice was begun in the KR and carried through extremely rigorously in the version of Aquila.[9]

In the following paragraphs a synthetic presentation will be made of the available data concerning successive stages in the recensional development of the Greek text in Samuel and Kings. The purpose of this reconstruction is to provide clear and simple criteria for use in the textual analyses in subsequent chapters. Each of the four principal text types will be characterized briefly, together with its Hebrew *Vorlage*. The most important manuscripts for each text type will also be listed.

The Old Greek

Characteristics. As noted in the Introduction,[10] Thackeray was the first to divide the Greek text of Samuel and Kings as found in the Codex Vaticanus (B) and the majority of the other Greek manuscripts into two sections that he considered to be the work of two distinct translators. Barthélemy has revised Thackeray's hypothesis and has shown that in the four Books of Samuel and Kings the so-called Septuagint does not represent the work of two translators, but rather two stages in the recensional development of the text: original translation and subsequent recension. This view has received confirmation from the recent study by Ilmari Soisalon-Soininen of the use of the infinitive in the Septuagint.[11] Barthélemy has further proposed that the revision of the original Greek translation of Samuel and Kings is but part of a more extensive recensional activity discernible in other OT books.[12]

Because the two sections of the Greek text in Samuel and Kings are distinguished by certain stylistic and lexical peculiarities, the characteristics of the Old Greek can be studied best in comparison with those of the subsequent recension (KR) for these same books. This comparison will be made later in the treatment of the KR.

Hebrew Vorlage. The description of the Hebrew text form underlying the successive stages of the evolving Greek text is derived from the history of Hebrew textual families elaborated by Cross.[13] Although the theory of local Hebrew text types is open to further refinement, the evidence presently available in support of this theory warrants its use as a working hypothesis that may serve as a starting point for further detailed research in a complex area.[14]

Corresponding to the Old Greek there was an Egyptian text type of the Hebrew. The latter text had already diverged from the Old Palestinian text type of the Hebrew, from which it was derived, by the time of the Old Greek translation in the third century B.C. The Egyptian Hebrew text may have begun its independent course of development in Egypt as early as the fourth century B.C.[15]

Textual Witnesses. The best witness in Samuel and Kings for the pre-hexaplaric text of the Old Greek is the Codex Vaticanus. This manuscript serves as the basic text for the Larger Cambridge Septuagint, from which Greek citations are taken throughout this study. Fortunately, the purity of this codex as a witness to a pre-hexaplaric text seems to be greatest precisely in the Books of Samuel and Kings.[16]

Aside from the Codex Vaticanus this text type is restricted to a small number of manuscripts.[17] The Codex Vaticanus does not exhibit the Old Greek translation throughout, however, but only in the following sections, which are arranged here according to the classification of Thackeray: I Samuel; II Samuel 1:1–11:1 (but see Appendix B); and I Kings 2:12–21:29.

The remaining sections of the text of Codex Vaticanus for Samuel and Kings belong to the KR. Other Greek manuscripts, which have undergone varying degrees of assimilation to the hexaplaric recension, had as their basis a pre-hexaplaric text exhibiting this same division between the Old Greek and the KR. The only exception is the small group of manuscripts displaying the Lucianic text.

Proto-Lucian

Characteristics. It has long been recognized that the text identified in certain Greek manuscripts as Lucianic is composed of two distinct strata. The first of these is an ancient text form dating back to the first centuries before the Christian Era.[18] The second stratum comprises the additions by means of which the ancient stratum was brought into partial conformity with the hexaplaric text.[19] Tradition, though vague about details, confers upon the martyr Lucian[20] the honor of having made this revision of the Antiochene text at the end of the third century after Christ, and perhaps of having added certain stylistic touches to the resultant text form.[21]

The debate over the nature and origin of the Lucianic text has been reopened by the recent publications of two scholars, Cross and Barthélemy, whose work is of prime importance because it is based upon the manuscript discoveries from the Judean desert. Their respective studies have led them to adopt radically divergent views on the origin of the Lucianic text.

The conclusions of Cross are based on his examination of ancient

Hebrew manuscripts from Cave IV at Qumran. Though these manuscripts have not yet received official publication, preliminary reports have been available for some time,[22] and new readings are discussed in a recent article on the history of the biblical text.[23] In these studies, Cross offers evidence from Qumran Hebrew manuscripts for readings that correspond to readings in the Lucianic text while diverging from both the Old Greek and the MT. These readings in the Qumran manuscripts are regarded by Cross as witnesses to a local text type of the Hebrew distinct from the Hebrew *Vorlagen* of both the Old Greek and the proto-Masoretic text.[24] This local text type reflects the Old Palestinian textual tradition, and it would have been toward conformity with this Hebrew text form that the Old Greek translation was revised in the proto-Lucianic recension.[25]

The principal contribution of Barthélemy to the study of the development of the Greek text has been the identification of the KR (see next section). But in his book containing the preliminary publication of the scroll fragments of a Greek text of the Minor Prophets,[26] Barthélemy also advances a number of original hypotheses touching on several important areas of Septuagint research.[27] Among these is his novel suggestion that the proto-Lucian stratum of the Lucianic text is nothing else but the Old Greek.[28] At Antioch a manuscript tradition of the Old Greek would have been preserved even for those parts of the Books of Samuel and Kings where a later recension was substituted for the Old Greek in all remaining manuscripts. However, this Antiochene text form inevitably suffered corruption and in the course of time was increasingly assimilated to the hexaplaric text.[29] Thus for Barthélemy there was neither a proto-Lucian recension of the Old Greek toward a developing Hebrew text, nor a late Lucianic recension on a par with those of Origen and Hesychius.[30] Hence Barthélemy proposes that the term "Lucianic recension" be dropped in future discussions of the Greek text because it represents for him one of the myths connected with Septuagint research that his book is meant to dissipate.

As a practical consequence of this identification of the Lucianic text with the Old Greek, Barthélemy is able to use the Lucianic text as a surrogate for the Old Greek where the latter is wanting in the Second Book of Samuel.[31]

In evaluating the positions of Cross and Barthélemy[32] on the origin and character of the proto-Lucian stratum in the Lucianic text, preference must be given to the views of Cross because of his discovery of a number of proto-Lucian readings in the Hebrew manuscripts from Cave IV at Qumran. On the basis of these readings from several OT books, but especially from the Books of Samuel, it is evident that the Lucianic text contains an ancient stratum reflecting a text form that is both an early stage in the development of the Greek text and yet one that is distinct from the Old Greek translation. Although a proto-Lucian text type that is extensively preserved has not been found among the scanty remains of Hebrew manuscripts for the Books of Kings at Qumran, it is reasonable to suppose that the history of the development of the text for Kings is substantially the same as for the Books of Samuel, considering the intimate relationship of these four books to each other in the Greek text.

There is some justification, nevertheless, for Barthélemy's methodological procedure in using the Lucianic text as a surrogate for the Old Greek in textual analysis that emphasizes the difference between the Old Greek and proto-Lucian, on the one hand, and the later Greek recensions on the other. Despite the demonstrable differences between the Old Greek and proto-Lucian in a number of readings, these two text types have much in common in comparison with Greek texts of a later provenience.[33]

In the first place, the fundamental order of the text in the Books of Samuel and Kings is the same in the Old Greek and proto-Lucian, in striking contrast to the arrangement of the text in the MT and the Greek recensions based on this latter Hebrew text type. An excellent illustration is I Kings. In the chapters (3–14) dealing with the reign of Solomon and the disruption of the United Monarchy, the order of the text in the MT is at wide variance from the order in the Old Greek.[34] The Lucianic text, however, coincides perfectly with the Old Greek in ordering of the text, whereas the late Greek recensions have been assimilated to the MT. A further illustration is the order of chapters 20 and 21, which is reversed in the MT in comparison with the Old Greek and the Lucianic text. In the important matter of chronology in the Books of Kings, proto-Lucian agrees with the Old Greek wherever the latter is extant. (This point will be discussed in detail in the following chapter.) In matters of Greek style, finally, the Old Greek and Lucianic texts stand in marked contrast to the later Greek recensions. Evidence for this assertion will be presented when the KR is characterized.[35]

Hebrew Vorlage. The proto-Lucian recension was probably made in the second or first century B.C.[36] The Old Greek translation was revised toward a developed Palestinian Hebrew text type.[37] It is not possible at the present stage of Septuagint research to determine the extent of the proto-Lucian recension for the whole of the OT text. However, because extensively preserved manuscripts of the Palestinian Hebrew text of the same type as the *Vorlage* of the proto-Lucian recension have been found at Qumran for both Books of Samuel, it is safe to conclude that the proto-Lucian text form is present as the basic stratum in the Lucianic text for the Books of Samuel and Kings.

Textual Witnesses. The manuscripts that have been identified with certainty as belonging to the Lucianic text for Samuel and Kings are the minuscules: boc_2e_2.[38] A number of other manuscripts have occasional Lucianic readings in the text or as marginal annotations.[39]

The Καίγε *Recension*

Characteristics. As mentioned earlier, the most notable contribution of Barthélemy to Septuagint research has been the identification of a new Greek recension. There had long been speculation concerning the existence of a proto-Theodotion translation or recension. Barthélemy has attempted to synthesize the pertinent data from many OT books on the basis of common translation characteristics. His designation for the new recension has been followed in this study because it is derived from a translation characteristic of the recension and does not prejudice the question as to the author or date of the recension.

The translation of the Hebrew םג by καίγε is the characteristic not only of the recension for which this Greek expression is used as a designation, but also of the two later versions, those of Aquila and Theodotion, both of which were based upon the KR. Barthélemy considers the version of Aquila to be the only version based on the KR because he identifies the author as Theodotion.[40] Although Barthélemy has shown that the attribution to Theodotion of the readings in the sixth column of the Hexapla for II Samuel is erroneous,[41] the same conclusion is not valid for the readings from the sixth column for II Kings. The readings ascribed here to Theodotion on the basis of the hexaplaric signs stand in the same relation to the text of the Codex Vaticanus, which here displays the KR, as the developed text does to its forerunner.

Barthélemy would call these two texts the first and second Palestinian recension.[42] If for him the first Palestinian recension equals Theodotion, then the second Palestinian recension should be called post-Theodotion. Actually there is nothing to be gained by this juggling with names. It is simpler to retain the designation Theodotion for the text in Origen's sixth column, unless there is positive evidence that the attribution is erroneous. The KR might then be considered either as proto-Theodotion or proto-Aquila, as it is the predecessor of both.

Apart from the question of authorship, Barthélemy's observations on the KR can be adapted readily to support the comprehensive hypothesis being outlined in this chapter for the development of the Greek text in Samuel and Kings. Barthélemy correctly emphasizes that the KR was a revision toward a Hebrew *Vorlage* of the same type as the MT.[43] Consequently the KR must follow the Old Greek and proto-Lucian in chronological sequence. But more will be said below of the Hebrew *Vorlage* of the KR.

The first characteristic, then, of the KR which distinguishes it from the Old Greek and proto-Lucian is its greater conformity to the MT. In the ordering of the text the KR follows the same pattern as the MT. Within many verses, however, there are still slight divergences from the MT that show that the Hebrew *Vorlage* of the KR was not yet the fully developed MT. In II Kings there are hundreds of hexaplaric alterations by means of which the text of the KR was assimilated to the MT.

The second distinguishing characteristic of the KR is that its translation technique reveals an extreme concern that at least certain important Hebrew expressions receive a uniform rendition into Greek even at the expense of sound Greek usage and idiom.[44] Thackeray compiled a list of stylistic and lexical criteria for determining the presence of this translation technique in the Books of Samuel and

Kings.[45] Barthélemy has built upon the work of Thackeray and extended the number of criteria.[46] A fresh examination of the old criteria of Thackeray has enabled Barthélemy to discover the existence of the KR outside the Books of Samuel and Kings and to conclude that there is question here of a genuine recension and not merely of an isolated translation technique.[47]

Although perhaps none of the criteria that Barthélemy proposes would be conclusive if taken singly, the concurrence of several of these criteria in a passage is adequate to identify it as belonging to the KR. Significantly for the present study, the place where these criteria of identification have been most clearly established is precisely in the Books of Samuel and Kings. Because the criteria proposed by Thackeray and Barthélemy can be consulted in the references given above, they will not be repeated here, but application will be made of them as occasion offers in the subsequent textual analyses.

In the following paragraphs two new stylistic criteria for determining the presence of the KR are proposed. As in the case of the other recensional characteristics, a Hebrew word or phrase is translated one way by the Old Greek and proto-Lucian and another way by the KR. The distribution pattern in Samuel and Kings for the new characteristics corresponds exactly to the distribution pattern for the translation characteristics already discovered by Thackeray and Barthélemy.

The first of the new criteria is the characteristic Greek rendition of the Hebrew phrase בעיני. This expression may be understood literally as "in the eyes of," or more abstractly, as "in the judgment of." In Samuel and Kings there are three words or phrases employed in translating the Hebrew expression into Greek: ἐν ὀφθαλμοῖς, ἐνώπιον, and ἐναντίον. The first two are used most frequently. Rahlfs has called attention to their importance for distinguishing between different translation techniques in the Books of Kings, although he did not relate his observations to the question of recensional development.[48]

In tabulating the occurrences of these Greek renderings of בעיני the Books of Samuel and Kings will be divided into major sections according to the scheme first proposed by Thackeray and also adopted by Barthélemy.[49] These sections in turn will be grouped under the text type to which they belong.

Chapter I

Old Greek	KR
α′ I Samuel	βγ′ II Samuel 11:2–I Kings 2:11
ββ′ II Samuel 1:1–11:1[50]	γδ′ I Kings 22:1–II Kings 25:30
γγ′ I Kings 2:12–21:43	

In the following tables the occurrences of בעיני have been divided into three categories for greater precision of analysis. The first numbers under each Greek word represent the number of times the Greek expression occurs in B, and the numbers in brackets represent the number of times the respective Greek renderings of בעיני occur in L (boc_2e_2). In three instances in the Books of Kings בעיני is transslated by the simple dative (I Kings 9:12; II Kings 7:2, 19).[51] To obviate circular reasoning the texts that will be examined in detail in succeeding chapters are left out of consideration in compiling these tables. Here and throughout this study the data of the MT have been derived from Solomon Mandelkern, *Veteris Testamenti Concordantiae Hebraicae atque Chaldaicae*, 5th ed. (Jerusalem, 1962); Greek data have been taken from E. Hatch and H. A. Redpath, *A Concordance to the Septuagint*, I, II, III (Oxford, 1897).

בעיני יהוה

	ἐν ὀφθαλμοῖς[52]	ἐνώπιον[53]	ἐναντίον[54]
α′	– [–]	3 [2]	– [1]
ββ′	– [–]	– [–]	– [–]
γγ′	– [–]	13 [13]	– [–]
βγ′	2 [–]	– [2]	– [–]
γδ′	24 [3]	5 [26]	1 [–]

בעיני־

+ pronominal suffix = Yahweh

	ἐν ὀφθαλμοῖς[55]	ἐνώπιον[56]
α′	– [–]	1 [1]
ββ′	1 [1]	1 [1]
γγ′	– [–]	2 [2]
βγ′	2 [–]	– [2]
γδ′	3 [3]	– [–]

בעיני־

+ pronominal suffix or noun
= someone other than Yahweh

	ἐν ὀφθαλμοῖς[57]	ἐνώπιον[58]	ἐναντίον[59]
α′	19 [17]	5 [9]	– [-]
ββ′	3 [2]	4 [4]	– [-]
γγ′	– [-]	1 [1]	1 [1]
βγ′	13 [6]	– [6]	– [-]
γδ′	3 [3]	– [-]	– [-]

In other OT books, especially Chronicles, ἐναντίον occurs more frequently than in Samuel and Kings. Because it is quite rare in these latter books, the following observations will be concerned with a comparison of the uses of the remaining two Greek expressions, ἐν ὀφθαλμοῖς and ἐνώπιον.

בעיני יהוה. In the Old Greek, ἐν ὀφθαλμοῖς is never used for this Hebrew expression. In sharp contrast is the practice of the KR, which uses ἐν ὀφθαλμοῖς in an overwhelming majority of instances, twenty-six out of thirty-two times. In I Kings most instances of the Hebrew expression are found in that part of the regnal formula where the Deuteronomic historian passes judgment on the king. This is the identical context for the occurrences of the Hebrew expression in the section of Kings corresponding to the KR. The only satisfactory explanation for the divergence in usage between the Old Greek and the KR sections is that the author of the KR has purposely endeavored to insure the uniform translation into Greek of this Hebrew expression, as in the case of the other recensional characteristics discussed by Thackeray and Barthélemy. Moreover, the KR redactor has characteristically chosen a translation that is more literal than that employed in the Old Greek.

In five of the twenty-eight instances where בעיני occurs in II Kings in the Hebrew, ἐνώπιον is used in the KR. The simplest explanation for these exceptions seems to be that the KR redactor was not thoroughly consistent in carrying out his systematic revision of the Old Greek. Such exceptions have been noted by Barthélemy for the other translation characteristics of the KR.[60]

בעיני־ + *pronominal suffix* = *Yahweh*. Although there are far fewer instances of this Hebrew expression than of the preceding one, the same pattern of usage is discernible. The Old Greek uses ἐν ὀφθαλμοῖς in only one out of five possible instances. (See Appendix B for the arguments that chapter 10 of II Samuel, in which this lone exception occurs, should be considered a part of the KR.) On the other hand, the KR employs ἐν ὀφθαλμοῖς exclusively.

בעיני־ + *pronominal suffix or noun* = *someone other than Yahweh.* For this third category of usage with בעיני the evidence of the Old Greek is not as unequivocal as for the preceding categories. In twenty-two out of thirty-three possible cases the Old Greek uses ἐν ὀφθαλμοῖς and employs ἐνώπιον in ten of the remaining instances and ἐναντίον only once. The KR, however, has perfect consistency, making use of ἐν ὀφθαλμοῖς in all sixteen possible cases.

Here the Old Greek is using ἐν ὀφθαλμοῖς in two thirds of all possible instances, whereas in the preceding two categories, when the Hebrew expression referred to Yahweh, it employed ἐν ὀφθαλμοῖς in only one out of twenty-one cases. It cannot be coincidence that this variation in translation practice of the Old Greek corresponds to the variation in reference of the Hebrew expression: to Yahweh in the first two categories and to humans in the third. It would seem that the Old Greek practice, then, was to employ ἐνώπιον when בעיני־ referred to Yahweh, and ἐν ὀφθαλμοῖς when the Hebrew expression referred to humans. It is most likely not a coincidence either that the expression used in referring to Yahweh was less literal than that used in referring to humans.

An excellent illustration of the distinction between the divine and human referents is a verse from the α′ section of the Old Greek (I Samuel 26:24):

והנה כאשר גדלה נפשך היום הזה בעיני כן תגדל נפשי בעיני יהוה ויצלני מכל
צרה.

Καὶ ἰδοὺ καθὼς ἐμεγαλύνθη ἡ ψυχή σου σήμερον ἐν ταυτῃ
ἐν ὀφθαλμοῖς μου, οὕτως μεγαλυνθείη ἡ ψυχή μου ἐνώπιον
Κυρίου, καὶ σκεπάσαι με. καὶ ἐξελεῖταί με ἐκ πάσης θλίψεως.

The referent in the first instance of בעיני־ is David, and accordingly ἐν ὀφθαλμοῖς is employed. In the second instance, the referent is Yahweh and the Old Greek uses ἐνώπιον.

It is also important to observe the pattern of usage in L. In the sections of Samuel and Kings where the Old Greek is extant the practice of L of employing ἐνώπιον and ἐν ὀφθαλμοῖς is almost identical to that of the Old Greek. This correspondence is not surprising considering the close affinity of the Old Greek to proto-Lucian, as remarked earlier. In the KR sections, however, the contrast is striking. To translate the expression בעיני יהוה in II Kings, the KR uses ἐν ὀφθαλμοῖς in twenty-three out of twenty-eight cases, whereas L employs ἐνώπιον in twenty-five out of twenty-eight instances. The translation practice of L is exactly what would have been expected for the Old Greek had it been preserved in these sections. As in the case of the other criteria for distinguishing the Old Greek from the KR, L displays the same translation characteristic as the Old Greek. In the three instances where L agrees with the KR in using ἐν ὀφθαλμοῖς when referring to Yahweh it is probable that later assimilation has taken place because L is represented only by a few cursive manuscripts and no longer has the support of the Old Greek in these sections.

The data for the second of the newly discovered translation characteristics are less complicated than for the first. The Hebrew verb זבח which occurs in Samuel and Kings thirty-nine times with the meaning "to sacrifice," is translated in the Old Greek and proto-Lucianic texts by the verb θύειν, whereas the KR employs the verb θυσιάζειν.

	θύειν[61]	θυσιάζειν[62]
α′	11 [14]	– [-]
ββ′	– [-]	– [-]
γγ′	10 [11]	– [-]
βγ′	– [4]	4 [-]
γδ′	1 [5]	7 [3]

In the Old Greek and Lucianic texts the normal translations for the noun זבח, meaning "sacrifice", and the noun מזבח, meaning "altar," were θυσία and θυσιατήριον, respectively. The KR redactor evidently wished to introduce a verb form (θυσιάζειν) that more closely resembled the two nouns θυσία and θυσιαστήριον. This translation practice of the KR redactor was subsequently followed in the versions of Aquila and Theodotion.

The preceding investigation has established that the respective Greek translations of the Hebrew phrase בעיני יהוה and the verb זבח

are reliable criteria for distinguishing the Old Greek from the KR in the Books of Kings. These two criteria have been discussed here because they will be employed in the textual analyses of the following chapter. For a list of additional translation characteristics see Appendix A.

Hebrew Vorlage. The Hebrew text type toward which the Greek was revised in this recension was much closer to the MT than were the *Vorlagen* of the Old Greek or proto-Lucian. In the ordering of the verses, the KR follows the same pattern as the MT. Within a given verse, however, there are still slight divergences from the MT which show that the Hebrew *Vorlage* of the KR was not yet the fully developed MT but a forerunner, which can be termed a proto-Masoretic text. As the Hebrew *Vorlagen* of the Old Greek and proto-Lucian represented distinct local text types (the Egyptian and Palestinian), so the proto-Masoretic Hebrew *Vorlage* of the KR was a development of the Babylonian local text type. The date of the KR may be put tentatively somewhere in the first century of the Christian Era.[63]

Textual Witnesses. As noted earlier, the majority of Greek Bible manuscripts, including the Codex Vaticanus, displays a text in Samuel and Kings that alternates between the Old Greek and the KR. The sections belonging to the KR in the Books of Kings are: I Kings 1: 1–2:11; 22; and all of II Kings with the exception of four verses: II Kings 1: 18[a–d]. These four verses will be examined in detail in the following chapter, where it will be shown that they are a vestigial remnant of the Old Greek translation of II Kings.

The Hexaplaric Recension

Characteristics. This is the latest of the major Greek recensions. Origen's intention was to make the Greek text chosen as the basis of his revision conform with the definitively established MT. To do this he borrowed at times from several late Greek versions in order to supply material wanting in the earlier text.

The principles governing Origen's textual revision are too well known to require repetition here.[64] The following remarks will be

confined to methodological observations on the relation of the hexaplaric recension in Samuel and Kings to the earlier recensions discussed
above.

The best manuscript of the Books of Samuel and Kings for both
the Old Greek and the KR is the Codex Vaticanus. The text displayed
by this manuscript is commonly conceded to be pre-hexaplaric, which
means that it, or a closely related text form, served as the basic text
for Origen's recensional activity. Subsequent infection of the Vaticanus
text by the hexaplaric recension has been negligible and is more
pronounced in II Kings than in I Kings.[65] When account has been
taken of these rare hexaplaric accretions to the Vaticanus text, it is
only necessary to compare Vaticanus with known hexaplaric texts in
order to determine the textual development from the Old Greek or
the KR to the hexaplaric recension in a given passage. The hundreds
of alterations, of course, made in these older Greek texts by the hexaplaric recension in the Books of Kings are always in the direction of
greater conformity to the definitive MT.

The Lucianic text has two strata: proto-Lucian and the elements
assimilating the earlier stratum to the hexaplaric recension. The
hexaplaric additions are often easily recognizable. Many times a
Lucianic manuscript will have one of the hexaplaric signs, thus explicitly indicating that a given reading is hexaplaric.[66] In the absence of
such signs, the coincidence of a reading in the Lucianic text with the
reading of the normal hexaplaric witnesses, when such a reading is
not found in the Old Greek or the KR, justifies the presumption that
the reading in question is an assimilation from the hexaplaric text
introduced into the proto-Lucianic text by a later redactor.

The late Greek versions of Aquila, Theodotion, and the so-called
Quinta will be considered here only in relation to the hexaplaric recension. The practical problem is to devise adequate criteria for
distinguishing the three texts — the KR, Aquila, and Theodotion —
that have in common the translation characteristics of the newly
discovered recension. The most obvious criterion is the presence of
the hexaplaric signs α′ and θ′, provided these are genuine, in the
hexaplaric manuscripts that also contain readings from the later
versions of Aquila and Theodotion. The unique trait of Aquila, moreover, is the practice of translating the Hebrew accusative particle את

by σύν. The rules governing Aquila's translation of the Hebrew
accusative particle have been worked out by Barthélemy, who shows
that the Homeric use of σύν as an adverb is at the base of Aquila's
translation technique.[67] Less pervasive translation traits of Aquila have
also been discovered.[68] Because the version of Theodotion was used
by Origen to bring the earlier text forms, including the KR, into
conformity with the developed MT, Theodotion's revision can be
distinguished from the KR, or proto-Theodotion, by its greater
fidelity to the MT.

Barthélemy believes that the so-called Quinta, extant in the Books
of Samuel and Kings only for II Kings, is the Old Greek translation.[69]
In stating this conviction he repeats a suggestion already made by
F. C. Burkitt.[70] Neither of these authors, however, has satisfactorily
explained how the Old Greek translation could have been used, as
they assert, along with the versions of Aquila, Symmachus, and
Theodotion, to bring the KR in II Kings into conformity with the
MT. The KR already represents a revision of the Old Greek toward
a proto-Masoretic text type. The difficulty arises because the Quinta
(ε') is often cited together with Aquila, Theodotion, and Symmachus
as a witness to a hexaplaric reading.

Hebrew Vorlage. The Hexapla is the only Greek text form among
those discussed in this chapter whose Hebrew *Vorlage* was the developed MT. The dependence upon the latter, however, may well be
only indirect, for it is not clear whether Origen revised his basic
Greek text against the Hebrew of his first column or against the Greek
versions of Aquila, Symmachus, Theodotion, and in II Kings, the
so-called Quinta also.[71] Origen's recension was made in the middle
of the third century after Christ, approximately a century after the
definitive stabilization of the MT.

Textual Witnesses. The best witnesses in Greek to the hexaplaric
text are the Codex Alexandrinus (A) and the minuscules c (only in
Samuel) and x.[72] Among the versions other than Greek, the Armenian
is consistently hexaplaric.[73] So too, of course, is the Syrohexapla,
which exhibits the hexaplaric signs and is well represented throughout
the Books of Kings.

Too little is known of the third of the great Christian recensions,
that of Hesychius, for it to have any practical import for the present

study.[74] The attempts of later Greek scribes to make sense out of the refractory chronological data of the MT by devising new chronological systems are not discussed in this chapter because they do not contribute to the understanding of the parallel evolution of the early Hebrew and Greek texts.[75]

The basic conclusions of the preceding survey that will guide the investigation of the chronological data of the Greek texts in subsequent chapters can be summarized as follows:

1. There are four major stages in the development of the Greek text in Samuel and Kings: the Old Greek, proto-Lucian, the KR, and the hexaplaric recension.

2. A stage in the parallel development of the Hebrew text corresponds to each of these stages in the development of the Greek text.

3. There are definite criteria for identifying these four major text types in the Greek manuscripts and for determining to which of them a given chronological datum is to be assigned.

4. Individual items of chronological data in the Greek text can be correctly evaluated only with reference to their context in the history of the parallel development of the Greek and Hebrew texts.

CHAPTER II

Chronologies
in the Books
of Kings

Of perennial interest to Old Testament research is the problem of chronology in the Books of Kings. New hypotheses are constantly advanced that aim at reconciling the disparate data of the biblical texts with each other, and with the synchronisms provided by ancient Near Eastern history, and yet no wholly satisfying system of biblical chronology has been devised. The present study is not just one more attempt to work out a consistent biblical chronology but is rather a fresh evaluation from a new methodological standpoint of all the biblical data upon which a fully satisfying chronology must be constructed.

Whatever the opinion held of the value of the chronological data supplied by the Greek texts in the Books of Kings, some account must be taken of them in any adequate treatment of the chronological problem. If, however, a view of the history of the development of the Greek and Hebrew texts as sketched in the preceding chapter is adopted, it is clear that the Greek chronological data would assume a much greater value; not as the reflection of the late and arbitrary tampering on the part of Greek scribes, but as the precious witness to a variant and conceivably more ancient Hebrew tradition. In the following discussion, then, the Greek chronological data will be studied as part of a textual tradition that possesses great significance in its own right, and not merely in comparison with the data of the MT, although constant reference will be made to the latter. And above all the Greek data will not be treated indiscriminately. At every point it must be determined to which of the four major text types a given chronological datum belongs. Only in this way can order be brought into the ostensibly conflicting Greek data, and a sound foundation be laid for meaningful comparison of the latter with the data of the MT.

Before beginning the examination of the Greek chronological data, certain preliminary observations must be made upon the chronological framework that is common to both the Greek and Hebrew texts in the Books of Kings.

The Chronological Framework

In the Books of Kings, the history of the divided monarchy is composed of two basic types of material.[1] The first comprises independent narratives of heterogeneous provenience most of which contain implicit reference to the chronology of the history of Israel and Judah.[2] The second type is a series of formal, stereotyped notices derived from the official archives of the two kingdoms. In the present study they have been designated as the regnal formulae.[3] They were meant to contain exact chronological data about the kings of Israel and Judah, as well as synchronisms for relating the reigns of one kingdom to those of the other. These regnal formulae were interwoven into the blocks of narrative material at what were considered the appropriate places, thereby lending a definite chronological consistency to the whole. One such large narrative sequence and its regnal formulae will be studied in a later chapter.

The Pattern of Regnal Formulae. In both the Greek and Hebrew texts, though with divergent results, the pattern of regnal formulae is constructed by the compiler according to the following principle with respect to the synchronisms.

> When the narrative of a reign (in either series) has once begun, it
> is continued to its close — even the contemporary incidents of a pro-
> phet's career, which stand in no immediate relation to public events,
> being included in it; when it is ended, the reign or reigns of the other
> series, which are synchronized with it, are dealt with; the reign over-

lapping it at the end having been completed, the compiler resumes his narrative of the first series with the reign next following, and so on.[4]

Because this principle of alternation from one series of kings to the other in the regnal formulae is observed by both the Greek and Hebrew chronologies, it is evident that a discrepancy of several years between the two traditions could very well involve a major dislocation in the order of the text, especially if the regnal formulae in question were embedded in a large block of narrative material. An example of this will be studied in the following chapter.

The Structure of Regnal Formulae. In subsequent textual analysis several regnal formulae will be the object of detailed examination. Because the generic, stereotyped elements in the regnal formulae are the most important for comparative study, these will now be enumerated. They are the same for both the Greek and Hebrew texts.

The regnal formula is composed of two parts, an introductory and a concluding formula. Between these two parts is inserted additional material having particular reference to the life and activity of the king whose reign is being treated. The regnal formula of Joash of Israel in the MT (II Kings 13: 10–13) is only an apparent exception to this practice.[5] The inserted material can vary in extent from several verses to several chapters. The introductory formula for the kings of Judah contains five elements:

1. a synchronism of the year of accession with the corresponding regnal year of the contemporary king of Israel;
2. the age of the king at accession to the throne;
3. the length of his reign;
4. the name of the Queen Mother;
5. a brief verdict, in deuteronomistic terms, upon the character of the king.

The introductory formula for the kings of Israel lacks the second and fourth of these elements. The verdict on the king of Israel is always unfavorable, being divided into a generic condemnation of the king and a specific indictment of his following in the footsteps of Jeroboam.

The concluding formula is identical for the kings of both Israel and Judah and comprises the following elements:

1. an indication of the source from which the information concerning the king was obtained, with the occasional addition of further details concerning the king's reign;
2. mention of the king's death and burial;
3. the notice of the due succession of the king's son.

Evidently this is an idealized schematization because all the above enumerated elements are rarely found in a single regnal formula. Good examples of complete regnal formulae with very little inserted material are the notice of Azariah (II Kings 15:1-7) for a king of Judah and the notice of Jehoahaz (II Kings 13:1-9) for a king of Israel.

Because of their stereotyped character the regnal formulae are of great methodological importance. They are found in sufficiently large number in both Books of Kings to allow for fruitful comparison of the different ways in which the same Hebrew expression is rendered by the different Greek text types. Assignment of a given chronological notice contained in a regnal formula to a specific text type will make it possible to determine the stage in the development of the Greek text, and consequently of its Hebrew *Vorlage*, at which the particular chronological item was adopted.

The Comparative Chronological Data

In presenting the comparative chronological data in the Greek and Hebrew texts no effort will be made here to determine systematically whether either kingdom employed antedating, postdating, or inconsequent accession-year dating, or whether the regnal year in either kingdom was Tishri–Tishri, or Nisan–Nisan, or some other possible arrangement. These subjects are discussed exhaustively by Thiele in a chapter devoted to the fundamental principles of Hebrew chronology.[6] Because the principles of the Hebrew scribes in dating the accession year of a king and the beginning of the regnal year must be derived from the chronological data of the Bible by inference, as they are nowhere stated explicitly, a given writer's understanding of these principles is intimately bound up with his total reconstruction of the biblical chronology, and not infrequently a great deal of circular reasoning is involved. Thiele's elaborate reconstruction is a good example of this. The validity of his fundamental principles depends upon the soundness of his total chronological system, which is based upon the gratuitous assumption of multiple coregencies and an exclusive reliance upon the chronological data of the MT.

The aim of the present inquiry is not to reconstruct a harmonious biblical chronology for which the distinctions mentioned in the preceding paragraph would be useful and even necessary but to demonstrate the relationship of divergent chronological data to different stages in the development of the textual tradition. For this purpose the explicit data of the biblical texts will suffice. On occasion, however, the distinctions referred to above will be utilized to elucidate certain problematical data.

From the point of view of agreement or disagreement between the Greek and Hebrew chronologies, the history of the divided monarchy falls into three major periods. These will now be discussed in the order of greatest agreement between the Greek and Hebrew traditions. The period subsequent to the fall of the northern kingdom needs no discussion because there are obviously no synchronisms for this period. At II Kings 21:1 the Lucianic manuscripts bo have the reading ten for the age of Manasseh at his accession to the throne, whereas the MT, the Codex Vaticanus (B), and the other Lucianic manuscripts have the reading twelve. Otherwise the three principal text forms agree with respect to the chronological data for this period.

The Period from Jehu to the Fall of Israel. There is no need to list all the data in detail. In the three major traditions (B, representing the KR; the Lucianic manuscripts boe_2; and the MT) there is complete agreement for all the chronological data contained in the synchronisms of the regnal formulae, with one exception.[7]

In the synchronism for Pekahiah at II Kings 15:23 the figure for the number of regnal years for Pekahiah is as follows in the various manuscripts:

MT B (and the minuscules not listed below): two

A boe_2r g: ten

N $c_2$defmnp*qstwz: twelve.

The MT and B do not represent independent witnesses, for it is expected that B, which displays the KR in this section of Kings, would have the same reading as the MT. The reading of the majority of the Lucianic manuscripts is supported by two other minuscules: r, which in II Kings is an excellent witness to L where extant; and g, which often displays L readings.[8] The text of Codex Alexandrinus, which is usually hexaplaric, follows here the Lucianic reading, as does the Armenian also.

This L reading is clearly incompatible with the remainder of the chronology which the Lucianic manuscripts, together with B and the MT, follow in this section of II Kings. At II Kings 15:27 the synchronism for Pekah in L is the fifty-second year of Azariah. This datum is in full accord with the number of regnal years (two) assigned to Pekah's predecessor, Pekahiah, in B and the MT, but not with the number for the regnal years (ten) in L. This latter variant at II Kings 15:23 has not therefore affected the L chronology as a whole because L at II Kings 15:27 has the same synchronism for Pekah as B and the MT, thus contradicting the figure it gave for the regnal years of Pekahiah.[9]

It is not impossible that the variant reading of L at II Kings 15:23 is a fossilized remnant of an ancient chronology. But because there are no further data concerning such a chronology, it seems pointless to speak of a Lucianic chronology for this period of the divided monarchy on the basis of an isolated variant reading.

One Lucianic manuscript, c_2, has a reading that agrees with a group of manuscripts that are the normal representatives of a minor and late Greek revision. These manuscripts, together with the minuscule v (which has omitted the whole synchronism at II Kings 15:23), have a sub-chronology for the difficult period in chapter 15. The agreement of the Lucianic manuscript c_2 with this late recension is coincidental, because c_2, which is otherwise characterized by its assimilation to the hexaplaric recension, has a unique and highly artificial chronological system. Because of the importance of the chronological data contained in the other Lucianic manuscripts (boe_2) it would be well at this point to give an explanation of the principles upon which the secondary and derivative chronology in c_2 has been constructed.

1. The greatest divergence among the various chronologies is to be found in the synchronisms rather than in the number of regnal years for the king. The number of regnal years for each king in c_2

agrees with the data of the MT with only five exceptions: Jehoram, Joram, Menahem, Pekahiah, and Pekah.

2. The reigns of Jeroboam and Rehoboam are considered to have begun at exactly the same time. All subsequent reigns are synchronized according to the method of dating known as inconsequent accession-year dating. The following comparison will illustrate how this method of reckoning differs from the two other methods of dating (accession-year dating and nonaccession-year dating) in use not only in Israel, but in the other kingdoms of the ancient Near East as well.

Nonaccession-year dating = antedating:
... last year of king A
    first year of king B ...
    (accession year)   (second year)

Accession-year dating = postdating:
... last year of king A
    (accession year)   first year of king B ...

Inconsequent accession-year dating:
... last year of king A
                first year of king B ...
                (accession year)

The artificial character of the inconsequent accession-year method of dating is evident. Unless every king were to die precisely on New Year's Day (whenever that may have been in the respective kingdoms) there would have been an interregnum after the death of every king during the unfulfilled part of his last year because the accession year of the new king is identical with the first full year of the new king and begins with the royal New Year.

3. Once this system of inconsequent accession-year dating has been set in motion by the redactor of c_2 on the basis of initial data supplied by the MT, it is carried out with absolute consistency. As a result the occasional agreements of c_2, now with the other Lucianic manuscripts, now with B, now with the MT, or finally, with other late Greek chronological systems, are purely coincidental. The following diagram

will illustrate the inconsequent accession-year method of reckoning of MS c_2. The top line gives the regnal years for Judah in continuous sequence, and the bottom line those of Israel.

```
                                                    Abijah
Rehoboam:  1 2 3 4 5 6 7 8 9 10 11 12 13 14 15 16 17  1  2  3
Jeroboam:  1 2 3 4 5 6 7 8 9 10 11 12 13 14 15 16 17 18 19 20


Asa:        1  2 3    4 5 6 7 8 9 10 11 12 13 14 15 16 17 18 19
Jeroboam:  21 22 1    2 1 2 3 4 5  6  7  8  9 10 11 12 13 14 15
                   Nadab Baasha


Asa:       20 21 22 23 24 25 26 27 28 29 30 31 32 33 34 35
Baasha:    16 17 18 19 20 21 22 23 24  1  2  1  2  3  4  5
                                         Elah  (Zimri)
                                               Omri


                        Jehoshaphat
Asa:       36 37 38 39 40 41  1 2 3 4 5 6 7 8 9 10 11 12 13 14 15
Omri:       6  7  8  9 10 11 12 1 2 3 4 5 6 7 8  9 10 11 12 13 14
                              Ahab


                                     Jehoram
Jehoshaphat: 16 17 18 19 20 21 22 23 24    25 1 2 3 4 5 6
Ahab:        15 16 17 18 19 20 21 22  1     2 1 2 3 4 5 6
                                    Ahaziah  Joram


             Ahaziah Athaliah   Jehoash
Jehoram:  7 8 9 10  1        1 2 3 4 5 6 1 2 3  4  5  6  7  8
Joram:    7 8 9 10 11        1 2 3 4 5 6 7 8 9 10 11 12 13 14
                            Jehu


Jehoash:   9 10 11 12 13 14 15 16 17 18 19 20 21 22 23 24 25
Jehu:     15 16 17 18 19 20 21 22 23 24 25 26 27 28  1  2  3
                                                    Jehoahaz


Jehoash:   26 27 28 29 30 31 32 33 34 35 36 37 38 39 40
Jehoahaz:   4  5  6  7  8  9 10 11 12 13 14 15 16 17  1
                                                    Joash
```

Amaziah:	1	2	3	4	5	6	7	8	9	10	11	12	13	14	15	16	17	18	19	20
Joash:	2	3	4	5	6	7	8	9	10	11	12	13	14	15	16	1	2	3	4	5

Jeroboam

Azariah

Amaziah:	21	22	23	24	25	26	27	28	29	1	2	3	4	5	6	7	8
Jeroboam:	6	7	8	9	10	11	12	13	14	15	16	17	18	19	20	21	22

Azariah:	9	10	11	12	13	14	15	16	17	18	19	20	21	22	23	24
Jeroboam:	23	24	25	26	27	28	29	30	31	32	33	34	35	36	37	38

Azariah:	25	26	27	28	29	30	31	32	33	34	35	36	37	38	39
Jeroboam:	39	40	41	1	2	3	4	5	6	7	8	9	10	11	12

(Zechariah
Shallum)
Menahem

Jotham

Azariah:	40	41	42	43	44	45	46	47	48	49	50	51	52	1	2	3	4	5
Pekahiah:	1	2	3	4	5	6	7	8	9	10	11	12	1	2	3	4	5	6

Pekah

Ahaz

Jotham:	6	7	8	9	10	11	12	13	14	15	16	1	2	3	4	5	6	7
Pekah:	7	8	9	10	11	12	13	14	15	16	17	18	19	20	21	22	23	24

Hezekiah

Ahaz:	8	9	10	11	12	13	14	15	16	1	2	3	4	5	?
Pekah:	25	26	27	28	29	30	1	2	3	4	5	6	7	8	9

Hoshea

In the above diagram the accession of Joram is synchronized with the first year of Jehoram at II Kings 1:18^a. In the regnal formula of Jehoram, however, at II Kings 8:16, which is not indicated in the above diagram, the accession of Jehoram is synchronized with the fifth year of Joram. This latter reading is in agreement with B, the MT, and the remaining Lucianic manuscripts. It is the only instance where c_2 has failed to revise the synchronism in the introductory part of the regnal formula. Even in the secondary chronological notices the c_2 redactor has carried out his systematic revision. For example, where the other text traditions assert that Amaziah lived fifteen years after the death of Joash (II Kings 14:17), c_2 has the number of years as fourteen. In addition to the synchronism of Hezekiah's accession with the corresponding year in the reign of Hoshea, there are two secondary synchronisms between these two reigns. The first of these (II Kings 18: 9) gives the synchronism for the beginning of the siege of Samaria by Sennacherib as the fourth year of Hezekiah equal to the seventh year of Hoshea. This is the reading of all textual traditions including c_2 and is in perfect accord with the latter's method of reckoning. The second sub-synchronism is the year of the fall of Samaria, which should be the sixth year of Hezekiah, equal to the ninth year of Hoshea, which is the reading of all the other text traditions at II Kings 18: 10. MS c_2 has the utterly anomalous reading of the tenth year of Ahaz, which makes no sense in the present context.

This excursus on the chronological system exhibited by the Lucianic manuscript c_2 has been necessary in order to make clear that the data of this manuscript are not to be accorded equal status with the chronological data of the other Lucianic manuscripts (boe$_2$) that for the most part preserve the Old Greek chronology. The chronological data of c_2 contribute nothing in fact to the determination of the early development of the Greek text. Apart from its late and artificial chronological system, however, c_2 is ordinarily a reliable witness to the Lucianic text, especially where it agrees with boe$_2$.

From a comparison of the principal textual traditions for the period from Jehu to the fall of the northern kingdom, the following conclusions can be drawn. Apart from the secondary chronological variants of such manuscripts as N defmpqstvwy and others, which belong to a late Greek recension, and the singular Lucianic manuscript c_2, the major traditions in both the Hebrew and Greek have an identical chronology for the period under discussion, with the single exception noted earlier: the number of regnal years for Pekahiah at II Kings 15: 23. Not only is there no distinct Lucianic chronology for this period, but there is no evidence for an early independent Greek chronology at all.

The Period from Jeroboam to Omri. The chronological data from the three principal textual traditions are given in the following table. The data of the Old Greek (B) and L (boe$_2$) are cited together. The capital letter in parenthesis after the name of the king indicates whether he is from Israel (I) or Judah (J). All chapter and verse references are to I Kings.

King	Regnal Years		Synchronisms	
	MT	B and L	MT	B and L
1. Jeroboam (I) (14:20)	22	—	—	—
2. Rehoboam (J) (14:21)	17		—	—
3. Abijah (J) (15:1–2)	3	6	18th of Jeroboam	
4. Asa (J) (15:9–10)	41		20th of Jeroboam	24th of Jeroboam
5. Nadab (I) (15:25)	2		2nd of Asa	
6. Baasha (I) (15:33)	24		3rd of Asa	
7. Elah (I) (16:8)	2		26th of Asa	[20th of Asa (16:6)]
8. Zimri (I) (16:15)	7 days (B: 7 years)		27th of Asa	(be$_2$: 22nd of Asa)
9. Omri (I) (16:23)	12		31st of Asa	

1. For Jeroboam, of course, there is no synchronism, but the MT gives the number of his regnal years. The section in the Hebrew text in which this latter notice is found (I Kings 14:1–20) has no counterpart in the Old Greek or Lucianic texts. The equivalent in the latter texts is to be found in the long doublet after I Kings 12:24, where the additional verses are designated 12:24[a–z] in the Larger Cambridge Septuagint. The narrative concerning the sickness of Jeroboam's child (14:1–18) is contained in more or less the same form in verses 12:24[g–n]. It can be demonstrated on stylistic grounds that the doublet 12:24[a–z], whatever its literary merits, belongs to an early stage of the development of the Greek text.[10] Some of the material it contains is to be found elsewhere in the Old Greek text, but the narrative in 12:24[g–n] in found only in this doublet, which may explain why the doublet was preserved in B and the Lucianic manuscripts.

The Hebrew text does not have the doublet at 12:24[a–z]. Correspondingly, the texts exhibiting the hexaplaric recension (Codex Alexandrinus, the Syrohexapla, and the Armenian) have omitted this section, as well as a group of Greek cursives representing a late Greek recension.[11] It is very significant that the aberrant Lucianic manuscript c_2 omits verses $12:24^{g-n}$. For in $14:1-20$ it is precisely c_2, along with the other hexaplaric witnesses, that in conformity with the MT includes the verses missing in the Old Greek and in L. It is also noteworthy that c_2 clearly marks with the asterisk this hexaplaric addition of twenty verses.

The manuscripts exhibiting I Kings $14:1-20$ are- A de(f)mp-tw-c_2 Armenian and Syrohexapla (sub * c_2 and Syrohexapla). A scholion in the Syrohexapla attributes these twenty verses to the version of Aquila.[12] This attribution is confirmed by the presence of the unmistakable translation characteristic in $14:8$, the rendition of the Hebrew accusative particle את by the Greek σύν.

Thus there is no conflict with the number of regnal years of Jeroboam at $14:20$ and the synchronism at $15:9$ in the Old Greek and Lucianic texts. These texts do not give the number of regnal years of Jeroboam at $14:20$, where the Greek text used in the hexaplaric recension is from the version of Aquila. In the doublet at $12:24^{g-n}$, which B and L do have, there is no chronological data corresponding to the synchronism at $14:19-20$ in the MT.[13]

The hexaplaric addition of twenty verses $(14:1-20)$ in c_2 is very instructive for the light it throws upon the singular chronology exhibited by this aberrant Lucianic manuscript throughout the Books of Kings. The starting point of c_2 is the MT data for the number of regnal years of Jeroboam (twenty-two) and of Abijah (three), which contradicts the data of the other Lucianic manuscripts and the Old Greek. According to these texts the regnal years of Jeroboam were at least twenty-four, as can be inferred from $15:9$, whereas those of Abijah were six $(15:1)$. Beginning with the data of the MT the redactor of c_2 constructed his unique chronology.

2. There is no synchronism for Rehoboam, and the same figure for the number of regnal years (seventeen) is found in all the major text traditions. At $12:24^a$, however, B gives the number of regnal years as twelve.

3. The first calculation of a synchronism is for Abijah. All the major traditions agree in fixing his accession in the eighteenth year

of Jeroboam. However, the MT, B and L differ as to the number of regnal years: the former assigning three, the latter six years. Here c_2 has the number three, as noted above, indicating its dependence upon the data of the MT.

4. In the Old Greek and Lucianic texts the synchronism for Asa occurs in two places. The second of these is the usual notice at the beginning of the regnal formula (15: 9), which is also present in the MT. The first synchronism, lacking in the MT and in Greek texts of the hexaplaric recension, is contained in the concluding formula for Abijah (15: 8) and gives the date of the latter's death. In both instances the Old Greek and Lucianic manuscripts have the same synchronism, the twenty-fourth year of Jeroboam, which fully accords with the six years of Abijah's reign. This double synchronism of the Greek texts is important, for it would seem to prove that the Old Greek and Lucianic texts were following the system of postdating for Judah at this period.

Thiele has failed to take into account the first synchronism (15: 8) in his presentation of the data of the Greek texts for this period.[14] The reason for this omission would seem to derive from his inadequate acquaintance with the Greek text. He reprints without alteration the comparative chronological data given in Burney's *Notes on the Hebrew Text of the Books of Kings*, pages xlii-xliv.[15] This table gives the MT, Septuagint, and Lucianic data in parallel columns, but from the standpoint of the MT. Thus the synchronism at 15: 8 in the Old Greek and Lucianic texts is not given, because it does not correspond to anything in the MT.

By ignoring the synchronism at 15: 8, Thiele is able to organize the remaining Greek data into a system of reckoning based on the principles of inconsequent accession-year dating.[16] But his reconstruction would have been impossible had he taken into account the synchronism at 15: 8.

This synchronism is unique in the Books of Kings in that it gives the syncrhronism of the death of a king: in this case, that of Abijah. The year of his death is fixed in the twenty-fourth year of Jeroboam. At 15: 9 the year of the accession of his son, Asa, is fixed in the same twenty-fourth year of Jeroboam. The combination of these two synchronisms certainly proves that the Old Greek and Lucianic texts were not using the system of inconsequent accession-year reckoning at this period, as Thiele maintains. His synchronism of the death of Abijah with the twenty-third year of Jeroboam is simply false and was arrived at by means of his reconstruction based upon inadequate data and not by consulting the Greek text.[17]

If the data of the two synchronisms at 15: 8 and 15: 9 are compared with the synchronism for Abijah's accession (15: 1), which is given as the eighteenth year of Jeroboam, it is clear that the principle of postdating was used in reckoning Abijah's and Asa's synchronisms:

									Asa		
			Abijah						(ac) 1 2 . . .		
			ac	1	2	3	4	5	6		
Rehoboam:	. . .	15	16	17							
Jeroboam:	. . .	16	17	18	19	20	21	22	23	24	. . .

By way of contrast, c_2 has the synchronism for the death of Abijah at 15: 8 as the twentieth year of Jeroboam, having altered the number to agree with the shorter length of Abijah's reign, three years, as in the MT. At 15: 9, the beginning of Asa's reign, it has the twenty-first year of Jeroboam. This discrepancy in the two synchronisms demonstrates conclusively that c_2 is following the method of calculation based on the principle of inconsequent accession-year reckoning.

			Abijah			Asa	
			1	2	3	1	
Jeroboam:	. . .		18	19	20	21	. . .

5–6. The Hebrew and Greek texts are in agreement on the date for the reigns of Nadab and Baasha in the synchronisms of the regnal formulae. This is also true for the supplementary synchronism at 15: 28, which gives the year of Baasha's slaying of Nadab. In both the Greek and Hebrew this is the third year of Asa, agreeing with the date for Baasha's accession in the regnal formula at 15: 33. c_2, however, has substituted its own figures for all three of the synchronisms in question and is followed by b at 15: 28 and 15: 33.

7. Beginning with the reign of Elah until the establishment of the new dynasty under Omri the details of the history of the northern kingdom are confused. This confusion is reflected in the Greek texts, which are defective in their chronological data.

For the reign of Elah there are two places for synchronisms, as in the case of Asa and Nadab above. The first of these is the concluding formula of Baasha (16: 6), where the succession of his son, Elah, is fixed in the Old Greek and Lucianic texts for the twentieth year of Asa. This synchronism is lacking in the MT. The second synchronism is found in the usual place at the beginning of the regnal formula (16: 8). In the MT the synchronism is fixed for the twenty-sixth year of Asa. The Old Greek and Lucianic texts have simply omitted the synchronism at this point.

8. The uncertainty concerning the historical situation in the northern kingdom reaches its height with the reign of Zimri, as reflected in the divergent data of the several texts. The MT allots the brief reign of seven days to Zimri at 16: 15. All the Lucianic manuscripts (boc_2e_2) concur in this figure. B, however, supported by a_2 and the Ethiopic, has the number of seven years, which appears to be based upon some error. B and the Lucianic manuscript o omit the synchronism for Zimri, which the MT fixes as the twenty-seventh year of Asa, both at 16: 15 and in the supplementary synchronism at 16: 10. The Lucianic manuscripts be_2 give the synchronism as the twenty-second year of Asa.

As far as the synchronism is concerned there is at least no conflict between the Old Greek and the major Lucianic tradition. It is difficult to reconstruct the earliest Greek chronology for this period because of the serious omissions in the principal manuscripts.

9. With the synchronism for the reign of Omri there is once more agreement among all the text traditions. However, this agreement is only superficial, because the Hebrew and Greek texts understand the number of regnal years (twelve) in two different senses, as will be explained in greater detail in the following section.

By way of summary the following observations can be made on the comparative chronological data in the period from Jeroboam to Omri. At two places there is a discrepancy amounting to several years between the Hebrew and Greek chronologies. The Old Greek and Lucianic texts exhibit a single chronology. As in the period from Jehu to the fall of the northern kingdom, there is no justification for speaking of a Lucianic chronology as distinct from that of the Old Greek.

The Period from Omri to Jehu. A comparison of the data in the major text traditions reveals that for this period there are two irreducible chronologies. The one is followed consistently in the MT, with but a single exception, as well as in the Greek texts based upon the MT. For this reason it is designated as the Hebrew chronology. The other chronology is represented by the Old Greek, as long as that text form is extant, as well as by L, with only one exception. Hence it is called the Old Greek chronology.

In I Kings, until the end of chapter 21, the Old Greek chronology is represented by B and L (boe$_2$). Beginning with chapter 22, however, there is a change of text form in B from the Old Greek to the KR. This change of text form involves a switch from the Old Greek chronology to the Hebrew chronology. Thus B exhibits the Hebrew chronology in chapter 22 of I Kings and throughout II Kings. By contrast L continues to follow the Old Greek chronology in chapter 22 of I Kings and also in II Kings until the end of the period under discussion, with a single exception. This is the synchronism in the regnal formula of Jehoram of Judah at II Kings 8:16, where L has adopted the synchronism of the Hebrew chronology, thereby creating a conflict with the data of the Old Greek chronology, which L has otherwise preserved intact. It is possible, though, by extrapolation to conjecture what the synchronism for Jehoram would have been in the Old Greek chronology. In the following table the reconstructed synchronism and number of regnal years for Jehoram is enclosed in brackets. To minimize the confusion occasioned by the identical names of the kings of Judah and Israel who were contemporaries during this period, the name of the king of Judah is spelt Jehoram and the name of the king of Israel is spelt Joram.

The first item in the Old Greek chronology appears to be in perfect accord with the first notice in the Hebrew chronology. In both chronologies the regnal formula of Omri comes at the same place in the text (I Kings 16:23); there is the same synchronism for his reign, the thirty-first of Asa; and the same number of years duration to his reign, twelve. But underlying this seeming conformity is a radical divergence in the understanding of the number for the regnal years of Omri in the two chronologies. This discrepancy becomes apparent when the regnal formula for Omri is compared with the second regnal formula in both chronologies.

Chapter II

King	Regnal Years	Synchronisms
Old Greek Chronology		
I Kings 16: 23 Omri (I)	12	31st of Asa
16: 28ᵃ Jehoshaphat (J)	25	11th of Omri
16: 29 Ahab (I)	22	2nd of Jehoshaphat
22: 52 Ahaziah (I)	2	24th of Jehoshaphat
II Kings 8: 16 Jehoram (J)	[11?	2nd of Ahaziah?]
1: 18ᵃ Joram (I)	12	2nd of Jehoram
8: 25 Ahaziah (J)	1	11th of Joram
Hebrew Chronology		
I Kings 16: 23 Omri (I)	12	31st of Asa
16: 29 Ahab (I)	22	38th of Asa
22: 41 Jehoshaphat (J)	25	4th of Ahab
22: 52 Ahaziah (I)	2	17th of Jehoshaphat
II Kings 3: 1 Joram (I)	12	18th of Jehoshaphat
8: 16 Jehoram (J)	8	5th of Joram
8: 25 Ahaziah (J)	1	12th of Joram

According to the Old Greek chronology the first ten years of Omri's reign coincide with the final ten years of Asa, king of Judah. The latter is succeeded by Jehoshaphat, whose accession is synchronized with the eleventh year of Omri. There is thus an overlap in the reigns of Omri and Jehoshaphat. The Old Greek chronology has taken the number twelve in the figure for the regnal years literally as meaning that Omri reigned for twelve years as king of Israel, beginning in the thirty-first year of Asa. This is the obvious meaning of the data and the way in which the other numbers for regnal years are understood elsewhere in the Books of Kings.

This cannot be the understanding, however, of the number twelve in the Hebrew chronology. The second regnal formula in the Hebrew chronology states that Ahab succeeded Omri in the thirty-eighth year of Asa. By any method of calculation the period from the thirty-first of Asa, the accession year of Omri, to the thirty-eighth of Asa, the accession year of Ahab, cannot equal twelve years. The Hebrew chronology in assigning the number twelve as the figure for the regnal years of Omri must have intended to include in it a period of years before the official accession of Omri as king of Israel, or else there is a patent absurdity.[18]

In the period from Jeroboam to Omri discussed earlier, the confusion in the reigns of Elah, Zimri and, Omri, as reflected in the chronological data for these reigns, is noticeable. When the usurper Zimri assassinated Elah and assumed the rule over Israel in Tirzah, the Israelite army that was besieging Philistine Gibbethon proclaimed their commander, Omri, to be king. The latter promptly marched against Tirzah, precipitating the suicide of Zimri after a week in power (I Kings 16: 9–19). But Omri did not immediately succeed to undisputed hegemony over Israel. The people were divided between Omri and Tibni the son of Ginath. After several years of internecine strife the faction of Omri got the upper hand, Tibni was slain, and Omri became the sole ruler of Israel. Not long thereafter he purchased the hill of Shemer and transferred his capital to the new city of Samaria, which he built there (I Kings 16: 21–24).

According to the reckoning of the Old Greek chronology, the four

years from the death of Zimri to the death of Tibni, when Omri
was king in the eyes of the faction supporting him but not yet sole
ruler, are assigned to Tibni, although he is not listed officially among
the kings of Israel. That the Old Greek chronology considered Omri
to have begun his reign after Tibni is borne out by an extremely
important notice in the Old Greek and Lucianic texts at 16: 22. All
text forms have the following phrase at the end of verse 22: "And
Omri began to reign." But the Old Greek and Lucianic texts have
in addition to this phrase the words: "after Tibni" (μετὰ Θαμνεί).
These words are omitted in the MT and are under the obelus in the
hexaplaric recension. It is clear from the notice contained in the Old
Greek and Lucianic texts that the Old Greek chronology regarded
the four years after the death of Zimri not as an interregnum that
could be credited to Omri, but as the regnal years of Tibni, even
though his reign was not included in the official list of Israelite kings. [19]

In the Hebrew chronology the four years after the death of Zimri
are reckoned as part of the total of regnal years for Omri. It should
be observed that this procedure of reckoning the years before a
king's official accession as part of his regnal years is completely anomalous, having no parallel elsewhere in Kings. The case of coregencies,
even if they can be proved to have existed, is not a valid parallel.
No attempt will be made at this point to determine which chronology
is objectively superior: the Greek, which regards the twelve years of
Omri's reign to have begun with his official accession as sole ruler of
Israel in the thirty-first year of Asa, or the Hebrew, which considers
apparently that Omri's reign as king began when he was proclaimed
king by acclamation upon the assassination of Elah in the twenty-
seventh year of Asa. [20] It is enough for the present to have indicated
where the source of discrepancy lies between the two chronologies for
this period. In a subsequent chapter it will be shown that the reckoning
of the Hebrew chronology was secondary, and the reason for the alteration of the data of the older Greek chronology will be assigned.

The period of four years, more or less, that constitutes the discrepancy between the two chronologies at the beginning of this section
of Israelite history is significant first of all because it entails an alteration in all the synchronisms that follow. The two chronologies are
only made to coincide by the simultaneous slaying of Joram of

Israel and Ahaziah of Judah by a new Israelite usurper, Jehu. But in addition to the divergent synchronisms the variation of four years in the chronology also entails a divergence in the order of the text itself. In the discussion of the pattern of regnal formulae, it was observed that the principle of alternation between the two series of kings in Israel and Judah was followed by both the Greek and Hebrew chronologies. Thus for the period under consideration the last king of Judah to be mentioned was Asa, whose accession was synchronized with the last year of Jeroboam of Israel in either chronology. All the kings of Israel from Nadab to Omri had their accession years synchronized with the reign of Asa. This Israelite series should be continued until the reign of an Israelite king overlaps with the reign of Asa's successor, and then the compiler of Kings would be obliged to shift back to the series of Judean kings.

According to the Hebrew chronology, Ahab's accession year is also synchronized with the reign of Asa because in the Hebrew chronology Omri's reign of only seven years as sole ruler leaves an overlap of several years between the reigns of Ahab and Asa. Hence the regnal formula of Ahab must follow the regnal formula of Omri, and this is the order in the MT.

According to the Greek chronology, the twelve years of sole rule of Omri, beginning with the thirty-first year of Asa, would necessarily mean that Omri outlived Asa, whose regnal years are forty-one according to all traditions and that his reign would overlap with that of Asa's successor. Hence, according to the principle of the alternation of series, the regnal formula of Asa's successor, Jehoshaphat, would have to follow that of Omri, and this is the order in the Old Greek and Lucianic texts.[21]

Even admitting that the Greek chronology is following some principle in placing the regnal formula of Jehoshaphat at this place in the text, it could still be argued that this was a late insertion on the part of the Greek redactor and that the regnal formula of Jehoshaphat was taken from its proper place at I Kings 22:41, as in the MT, and inserted at I Kings 16:28[a] in accordance with a late Greek reworking of the chronology. The further fact that B gives the regnal formula for Jehoshaphat twice, at I Kings 22:41 and 16:28[a], would seem to support the view that the Greek text at one time followed the Hebrew

chronology and that later a doublet was inserted in the text in accordance with a newly devised Greek chronology.[22] Because the doublet
regnal formula of Jehoshaphat in the Greek text is of central importance to the present inquiry, a separate chapter will be devoted to
a detailed examination of it.

CHAPTER III

The Regnal Formula
of Jehoshaphat

Until now scholars have been unable to reach a convincing solution to the problem of the doublet regnal formula of Jehoshaphat in the Greek text. But the new understanding of the recensional development of the Greek text provides the necessary criteria for determining which of the two regnal formulae of Jehoshaphat in the Greek text is original and which secondary.[1] Following is a summary of the steps in the development of the present text in Codex Vaticanus.

1. In the Old Greek text the regnal formula of Jehoshaphat followed that of Omri at I Kings 16:28[a–h], in accord with the Old Greek chronology. The numeration of the Larger Cambridge Septuagint is misleading here because it is based on the MT and gives the impression that there has been an insert between verses 28 and 29. The regnal formula of Jehoshaphat is exactly where it is supposed to be according to the principle for the alternation of series. It has, moreover, the characteristic features, stylistic and lexical, of the Old Greek text, which prove that it cannot have been a late composition but must be original. The Lucianic manuscripts concur with the Old Greek here in every particular.

2. In chapter 22 of B the Old Greek text has been replaced by the KR and the regnal formula for Jehoshaphat has been inserted at verses 41–51 in conformity with the MT. These verses of the regnal formula have all the characteristics of the KR and evidently are a reworking of the earlier regnal formula at 16:28[a–h] with a view to bringing the latter into conformity with the proto-Masoretic text. The

presence of the regnal formula of Jehoshaphat at 22: 41–51 violates the principle of the alternation of series for the Old Greek chronology but is in perfect accord with the Hebrew chronology. Further evidence that the regnal formula of Jehoshaphat is a late insertion at 22: 41–51 is the omission of the regnal formula at this place in the text by all the Lucianic manuscripts, which thus preserve the Old Greek chronology throughout I Kings.

3. The patent contradiction in the Vaticanus text resulting from the juxtaposition of two text forms, and hence two different chronologies, is left unresolved because both regnal formulae of Jehoshaphat are preserved in B. This preservation may have been due to a reluctance on the part of the KR redactor to excise any part of the older text, even when it was at variance with his new chronology. Another example of this tendency will be seen in II Kings. The hexaplaric recension, however, had no such scruple because the original regnal formula of Jehoshaphat in the Old Greek text at 16:28[a–h] is omitted in Codex Alexandrinus, the Armenian and the Syrohexapla, making the text conform with the MT.

The accuracy of the preceding reconstruction may now be tested by submitting the pertinent texts to a detailed text-critical analysis. To facilitate comparison the verses in the Hebrew text are divided into smaller phrases and numbered for ease of reference. A detailed commentary follows the presentation of the comparative texts, and the significant variants of the Lucianic manuscripts are noted there.

I Kings 16:28[a–h]   I Kings 22: 41–51

Verse 28[a]   Verse 41

Καὶ ἐν τῷ ἐνιαυτῷ	Καὶ Ἰωσαφὰθ	ויהושפט 1
τῷ ἑνδεκάτῳ	υἱὸς Ἀσὰ	בן אסא 2
ἔτει	ἐβασίλευσεν	מלך 3
τοῦ Ζαμβρεὶ	ἐπὶ Ἰουδά	על יהודה 4
βασιλεύει	ἔτει	בשנת 5
Ἰωσαφὰθ	τετάρτῳ	ארבע 6
υἱὸς Ἀσά	τῷ Ἀχαὰβ	לאחאב 7
βασιλεύει	ἐβασίλευσεν	מלך ישראל 8

I Kings 16:28 [a–h]	I Kings 22:41–51	
	Verse 42	
	’Ιωσαφὰθ	יהושפט 1
ἐτῶν τριάκοντα	υἱὸς τριάκοντα	בן שלשים 2
καὶ πέντε	καὶ πέντε ἐτῶν	וחמש שנה 3
ἐν τῇ βασιλείᾳ αὐτοῦ	ἐν τῷ βασιλεύειν αὐτόν	במלכו 4
καὶ εἴκοσι	καὶ εἴκοσι	ועשרים 5
πέντε ἔτη	καὶ πέντε ἔτη	וחמש שנה 6
βασιλεύει	ἐβασίλευσεν	מלך 7
ἐν ’Ιερουσαλήμ	ἐν ’Ιερουσαλήμ	בירושלם 8
καὶ ὄνομα	καὶ ὄνομα	ושם 9
τῆς μητρὸς αὐτοῦ	τῇ μητρὶ αὐτοῦ	אמו 10
Γαβουζά	’Αζαεβὰ	עזובה 11
θυγάτηρ Σελεεί	θυγάτηρ Σεμεεί	בת שלחי 12

Verse 28 [b]	Verse 43	
καὶ ἐπορεύθη	καὶ ἐπορεύθη	וילך 1
ἐν τῇ ὁδῷ ’Ασὰ	ἐν πάσῃ ὁδῷ ’Ασὰ	בכל דרך אסא 2
τοῦ πατρὸς αὐτοῦ	τοῦ πατρὸς αὐτοῦ	אביו 3
καὶ οὐκ ἐξέκλινεν	οὐκ ἐξέκλινεν	לא סר 4
ἀπ’ αὐτῆς	ἀπ’ αὐτῆς	ממנו 5
τοῦ ποιεῖν τὸ εὐθὲς	τοῦ ποιῆσαι τὸ εὐθὲς	לעשות הישר 6
ἐνώπιον Κυρίου	ἐν ὀφθαλμοῖς Κυρίου	בעיני יהוה 7

	Verse 44	
πλὴν τῶν ὑψηλῶν	πλὴν τῶν ὑψηλῶν	אך הבמות 1
οὐκ ἐξῆραν	οὐκ ἐξῆρεν	לא סרו 2
	ἔτι ὁ λαὸς	עוד העם 3
ἔθυον	ἐθυσίαζεν	מזבחים 4
ἐν τοῖς ὑψηλοῖς	καὶ ἐθυμίων	ומקטרים 5
καὶ ἐθυμίων	ἐν τοῖς ὑψηλοῖς	בבמות 6

Verse 28 [c]	Verse 45	
καὶ ἃ συνέθετο	καὶ εἰρήνευσεν	וישלם 1
’Ιωσαφάθ	’Ιωσαφάθ	יהושפט 2
	μετὰ βασιλέως	עם מלך 3
	’Ισραήλ	ישראל 4

I Kings 16:28 a–h	I Kings 22:41–51	
	Verse 46	
	καὶ τὰ λοιπὰ	ויתר 1
	τῶν λόγων	דברי 2
	Ἰωσαφὰθ	יהושפט 3
καὶ πᾶσα δυναστεία	καὶ αἱ δυναστεῖαι αὐτοῦ	וגבורתו 4
ἣν ἐποίησεν	ὅσα ἐποίησεν	אשר עשה 5
καὶ οὓς ἐπολέμησεν		ואשר נלחם 6
οὐκ ἰδοὺ ταῦτα	οὐκ ἰδοὺ ταῦτα	הלא הם 7
γεγραμμένα	ἐνγεγραμμένα	כתובים 8
ἐν βιβλίῳ	ἐν βιβλίῳ	על ספר 9
λόγων τῶν ἡμερῶν	λόγων	דברי הימים 10
τῶν βασιλέων Ἰούδα	Ἰωσαφάθ	למלכי יהודה 11

Verse 28ᵈ	Verse 47	
καὶ τὰ λοιπὰ	[και περισσον	ויתר 1
τῶν συμπλοκῶν	του ενδιηλλαγμενου	הקדש 2
ἃς ἐπέθεντο	ουχ υπελειφθη	אשר נשאר 3
ἐν ταῖς ἡμέραις Ἀσὰ	εν ημεραις Ασα	בימי אסא 4
τοῦ πατρὸς αὐτοῦ	πατρος αυτου	אביו 5
ἐξῆρεν	επελεξεν	בער 6
ἀπὸ τῆς γῆς	απο της γης	מן הארץ 7

Verse 28ᵉ	Verse 48	
καὶ βασιλεὺς οὐκ ἦν	και βασιλευς ουκ ην	ומלך אין 1
ἐν Συρίᾳ	εν Εδωμ	באדום 2
νασεὶβ	εστηλωμενος	נצב 3
ὁ βασιλεύς	και ο βασιλευς	מלך 4

Verse 28ᶠ	Verse 49	
	Ιωσαφατ	יהושפט 1
ἐποίησεν	εποιησεν	עשר 2
ναῦν εἰς Θαρσεὶς	νηας	אניות תרשיש 3
πορεύεσθαι	του πορευθηναι	ללכת 4
εἰς Σωφείρ	ωφειρδε	אופירה 5
πορεύεσθαι ἐπὶ τὸ χρυσίον	εις χρυσιον	לזהב 6
καὶ οὐκ ἐπορεύθη	και ουκ επορευθησαν	ולא הלך 7

I Kings 16:28 [a-h]	I Kings 22:41–51	
ὅτι συνετρίβη	οτι συνετριβησαν	8 כי נשברה
ἡ ναῦς	νηες	9 אניות
ἐν Γασιὼν Γάβερ	εν Ασεων Γαβερ	10 בעציון גבר

Verse 28 [g]	Verse 50	
τότε εἶπεν	τοτε ειπεν	1 אז אמר
βασιλεὺς	Οχοζιας	2 אחזיהו
Ἰσραὴλ	υιος Αχααβ	3 בן אחאב
πρὸς Ἰωσαφάθ	προς Ιωσαφατ	4 אל יהושפט
ἐξαποστελῶ	πορευθετωσαν	5 ילכו
τοὺς παῖδάς σου	δουλοι σου	6 עבדי
καὶ τὰ παιδάριά μου	μετα των δουλων μου	7 עם עבדיך
ἐν τῇ νηί	και ταις ναυσιν	8 באניות
καὶ οὐκ ἐβούλετο	και ουκ ηθελησεν	9 ולא אבה
Ἰωσαφάθ	Ιωσαφατ]	10 יהושפט

Verse 28 [h]	Verse 51	
καὶ ἐκοιμήθη	καὶ ἐκοιμήθη	1 וישכב
Ἰωσαφὰθ		2 יהושפט
μετὰ τῶν πατέρων αὐτοῦ	μετὰ τῶν πατέρων αὐτοῦ	3 עם אבתיו
	καὶ ἐτάφη	4 ויקבר
		5 עם אבתיו
ἐν πόλει Δαυείδ	ἐν πόλει Δαυεὶδ	6 בעיר דוד
	τοῦ πατρὸς αὐτοῦ	7 אביו
καὶ ἐβασίλευσεν Ἰωράμ	καὶ ἐβασίλευσεν Ἰωράμ	8 וימלך יהורם
υἱὸς αὐτοῦ ἀντ' αὐτοῦ	υἱὸς αὐτοῦ ἀντ' αὐτοῦ	9 בנו תחתיו

In the following commentary the order of the MT is followed. The numbers in each verse correspond to the subdivisions of the Hebrew text. The primary interest in the investigation is in the characteristic differences between the Old Greek (OG) and the KR in the rendition of the stereotyped elements of the regnal formula.

Verse 41

The most obvious difference between the two Greek texts in this verse is in the order of the wording of the text.

1 and 2. The MT and the KR begin with the name of the king

first, whereas the Old Greek has the more common order in the regnal formulae of beginning with the synchronism.

In addition to the regnal formula under consideration, there are twenty-eight regnal formulae which have synchronisms, as well as two supplementary synchronisms closely related to the regnal formulae (II Kings 1: 17; 9: 29). In the first period of Israelite history discussed earlier (from Jehu to the fall of Samaria), the regnal formulae begin with the synchronism first fourteen times, and only once with the name of the king first, in both the Greek and Hebrew texts.[2]

In the period from Jeroboam to Omri inclusive, the regnal formulae begin with the name of the king first only once in all textual traditions. The synchronism comes first in the other six regnal formulae, although the synchronism has simply been omitted in the Old Greek at I Kings 16: 8, 15.[3]

In the period under discussion, comprising the regnal formulae from Jehoshaphat to Ahaziah of Judah and the two supplementary synchronisms, there is a significant divergence in practice between the Greek and Hebrew traditions, as the following indicates:

Synchronism first			*Name of king first*		
I Kings 16: 28[a]	Jehoshaphat	OG L	I Kings 22: 41	Jehoshaphat	MT KR
I Kings 16: 29	Ahab	OG L	I Kings 16: 29	Ahab	MT
I Kings 22: 52	Ahaziah (I)	L	I Kings 22:52	Ahaziah (I)	MT KR

The diversity in the structuring of the introductory part of the regnal formulae in these three instances is certain proof that a different Hebrew *Vorlage* underlay the Old Greek and proto-Lucianic texts than that represented by the MT and the KR.

There is a triple synchronism for the reign of Joram. It will be studied in detail in the next chapter. In all its forms (MT, L at II Kings 1:17; OG, L at II Kings 1:18[a]; MT, KR, L at II Kings 3:1) it has the less common order of the name of the king first. The last three synchronisms in this section (II Kings 8: 16; 8: 25; 9: 29) revert to the usual pattern of having the synchronism first.

Not only is the location of the synchronism in the regnal formula important but also the way in which the stereotyped Hebrew expression for the synchronism is rendered in the different Greek texts. In Kings there are two formulae for expressing the synchronisms in Hebrew:

Expression A	בִּשְׁנַת [year] (שְׁנָה)
Expression B	בַּשָּׁנָה ה [year]

The synchronisms in all the regnal formulae of both Books of Kings are formulated according to expression A. The additional שׁנה occurs at I Kings 16: 8, 15, 23, 29; II Kings 8: 25; 13: 1, 10; 14: 23; 15: 1, 8, 13, 17, 23, 27; 16: 1. In the supplementary synchronisms outside the regnal formulae both expressions A and B are used.

These two Hebrew expressions are rendered by four expressions in Greek:

I. ἐν ἔτει [year] (ἔτει)
II. ἐν τῷ ἔτει τῷ [year]
III. ἐν τῷ [year] ἔτει
IV. ἐν τῷ ἐνιαυτῷ τῷ [year]

Only expression I is used in the KR sections of Kings to translate Hebrew expression A in the synchronisms of the regnal formulae. The absence of the preposition ἐν in the synchronism of Jehoshaphat at I Kings 22: 41, the text under consideration, cannot be regarded as in any way typical but is probably due to defective transmission of the text. The superfluous שׁנה is rendered by an additional ἔτει in the Greek only at II Kings 13: 1, 10. The Syrohexapla translates this שׁנה more frequently (II Kings 13: 1, 10; 14: 23; 15: 1, 8), attributing the addition to Aquila and the Quinta at 14: 23, but no version seems to have translated the addition consistently.

To translate Hebrew expression A in the supplementary synchronisms the KR, employs Greek expression I (II Kings 9: 29; 15: 30; 17: 6; 18: 10; 24: 12), expression II (II Kings 25: 1) and expression III (II Kings 12: 6; 25: 27). At II Kings 25: 1, however, many Hebrew manuscripts, as well as the parallel in Jeremiah, chapter 52, have Hebrew expression B, so that expression II in the Greek most probably was a translation of a Hebrew *Vorlage* having expression B.

To translate Hebrew expression B, the KR employs Greek expression II (II Kings 11: 4; 18: 9). Two occurrences of Hebrew expression B are rendered by the Greek without the preposition ἐν (II Kings 19: 29 *bis*).

In the seven regnal formulae of the Old Greek where the synchronism is expressed, all four Greek expressions are employed: expression I (I Kings 15: 25; 16: 29) expression II (I Kings 15: 33; 16: 23); expression III (I Kings 15: 1); expression IV (I Kings 15: 9).

In the supplementary synchronisms Hebrew expression A occurs twice (I Kings 15: 28; 16: 10) but is only translated by the Old Greek at I Kings 15: 28, where expression I is used.

Hebrew expression B occurs three times in chapter 6 of I Kings. At 6: 1 the preposition ἐν is wanting in the Greek rendition; at 6: 37 expression II is employed; at 6: 38 the rendition is anomalous. For the remaining instances of Hebrew expression B, however, the Old Greek uses expression IV (I Kings 14: 25; 18: 1). The occurrence of expression IV in I Kings 22: 2, at the beginning of the KR section, must be regarded as due to the superficial revision of this chapter.

The results of this brief investigation can now be related to the text under discussion. In the synchronism of Jehoshaphat at I Kings 16: 28ª Greek expression IV is employed. This expression occurs elsewhere only in the Old Greek, once in another regnal formula (I Kings 15: 9) and in two supplementary synchronisms (I Kings 14: 25; 18: 1). In these latter instances Hebrew expression B (that is, with the use of the definite article twice) was evidently the Hebrew *Vorlage*. It seems likely from this comparison that the original Hebrew *Vorlage* of the regnal formula of Jehoshaphat at I Kings 16: 28ª, and perhaps also the regnal formula at I Kings 15: 9, had Hebrew expression B for the synchronism, in contrast to the MT where Hebrew expression A is always found in the synchronisms of the regnal formulae. Because Greek expression IV occurs elsewhere only in the Old Greek, and never in the KR sections of Kings in the synchronisms just examined, the presence of Greek expression IV in the text at 16: 28ª is conclusive proof that this regnal formula of Jehoshaphat belongs to the original Old Greek text. The additional ἔτει (only in B oa₂) is not part of Greek expression IV.

3. The word מלך offers the ideal criterion for distinguishing between the two Greek text forms: a Hebrew word that was undoubtedly the same in the Hebrew *Vorlage* of each Greek text, but

which was translated in a characteristically different way in each Greek text. The perfect of the Hebrew verb מָלַךְ is translated by the Greek aorist ἐβασίλευσεν in the KR, but by the Greek historical present βασιλεύει in the Old Greek. As a result of the studies of Thackeray and Barthélemy it has been established that the use of the historical present is one of the surest signs for distinguishing the Old Greek from the KR, especially in the Books of Samuel and Kings.[4]

Not all the evidence for this conclusion will be reviewed here, but the data concerning the one Hebrew verb in question will be examined. Quite evidently מָלַךְ is a verb of frequent occurrence in the regnal formulae of both Books of Kings and is thus an ideal word for comparative study.

In the KR sections of Kings מָלַךְ is never translated by the Greek historical present. In the eight regnal formulae, however, having a synchronism in the Old Greek section of I Kings, excluding of course the regnal formula now under discussion, the Greek historical present occurs eleven times in the B text as a translation of some form of the verb מָלַךְ.[5] The pattern of distribution in the Old Greek text is as follows:

βασιλεύει is used to translate the Hebrew perfect מָלַךְ six times in the expression of the synchronism at the beginning of the regnal formula.[6] The reason that it is wanting in the other two possible instances (16: 8, 15) is that the whole synchronism is missing in the Greek.

βασιλεύει is used in one instance to translate מָלַךְ where the latter expresses the duration of reign.[7] This is an exception to ordinary practice for elsewhere in these regnal formulae מָלַךְ in this sense is translated by the Greek aorist.

In four instances βασιλεύει is used to translate the Hebrew וַיִּמְלֹךְ in the concluding formula expressing the due accession to the throne of the legitimate successor.[8] Because there are only four occasions of normal succession in the eight regnal formulae in question, this translation practice is completely consistent.

The pattern of distribution in L is as follows. In the first two distribution patterns above, L is in complete agreement with the Old Greek. For the third class, however, L uses the aorist and not the historical present. It is thus more consistent than the Old Greek in that it employs βασιλεύει only to translate מלך and then only in specific instances.

L is more flexible than the KR in its translation of מלך in both Books of Kings, as might be expected. In four instances L renders the Hebrew perfect מלך by the Greek perfect βεβασίλευκεν, where the KR has mechanically translated by the aorist.[9] Because L is preserved in only five principal manuscripts and no longer has the support of the Old Greek as in I Kings, it is understandable that in II Kings the rare form of the historical present would gradually have become assimilated to the aorist, the only verb form used to replace the historical present by the predominant KR text form. However, as Barthélemy has observed, a number of instances of the historical present have survived in Greek texts other than B for II Kings, but especially in the Lucianic manuscripts. Barthélemy has compiled a list of these instances of the historical present.[10] Curiously, he has failed to mention in this list the survival of four instances of the Greek historical present for מלך as well as a number of other historical presents, as follows:

II Samuel	18: 7	πταίουσιν	L
		πίπτουσιν	L + z
I Kings	22: 52	βασιλεύει	L
II Kings	1: 18ᵃ	βασιλεύει	all except A
	4: 11	ἔρχεται	L + r
	5: 24	ἔρχονται	L
	6: 4	τέμνουσιν	bc₂e₂
	8: 24	θάπτεται	L + efmw
	10: 36+	βασιλεύει	L + r
	12: 1	βασιλεύει	bc₂ nxyᵇ
	13: 25+	θάπτεται	L + r

The result of this brief study of the Hebrew verb מלך can be succinctly summarized:

The Old Greek uses the historical present βασιλεύει eleven times in the regnal formulae to translate the verb מלך. In the same regnal formulae L employs the historical present βασιλεύει seven times. The KR levelled all the distinctions (historical present, aorist, perfect) observed in the Old Greek and L and translated both מלך and וימלך in the regnal formulae uniformly by the aorist.

Applying these data to the analysis of the text under discussion, it is reasonable to conclude that the presence of the historical present in the regnal formula of Jehoshaphat at I Kings 16: 28 [a] and its absence in the regnal formula of the same king at I Kings 22: 41 are clear proof that the former belongs to the original Old Greek text, and the latter to the KR.

4. The phrase ἐπὶ 'Ιουδά is in both the KR and the MT but is lacking in the Old Greek. The presence, however, of this phrase in L, and in the Old Greek elsewhere in the regnal formulae in I Kings (14: 21; 15: 1; 15: 9) suggests that the omission here in the Old Greek is due simply to textual disturbance.

5 to 7. There is no need to observe that the content of the synchronism in the two regnal formulae is completely divergent and that the two synchronisms reflect the Old Greek and Hebrew chronologies respectively.

The wording of the text in the KR conforms to the MT even to the extent of having the name of the king in the dative τῷ 'Αχαὰβ corresponding to the preposition ל in the MT לאחאב, whereas the Old Greek has the genitive in the name of the king: τοῦ Ζαμβρεί. Elsewhere in the synchronisms in the Old Greek the genitive is also used. In the KR sections of Kings the dative is employed as a rule. The word for king is always in the dative: βασιλεῖ. When the article precedes this noun it can be either in the dative, which of course is correct grammatically, or even in the genitive, a solecism that points to the incomplete revision of an older text form (cf. II Kings 15: 23, 27, 32).

8. For the first time in this verse the KR differs from the MT and goes rather with the Old Greek. Whereas the MT has the phrase מלך ישראל, which is expected in this context, the Old Greek and the KR have a verb, evidently reflecting the Hebrew verb מלך. The Old Greek renders this Hebrew verb characteristically with the historical present, whereas, the KR has the aorist. The agreement of the two Greek texts here in having a verb form, in opposition to the MT, suggests a hypothesis as to the relation of the two Greek texts that will have additional confirmation in succeeding verses. The regnal

formula in the KR is not a free creation of the KR redactor but a reworking of the regnal formula of the Old Greek text.[11] This reworking comprises three principal elements:

1. revision of the synchronism to accord with the Hebrew chronology rather than with the chronology of the Old Greek; 2. assimilation of the Old Greek text to the word order and phrasing of the MT; 3. substitution of characteristic translations for words that presumably had the same Hebrew *Vorlage* as in the MT.

These three steps in the adaptation of the earlier Greek text were not always carried out with perfect consistency by the KR redactor. The present instance is a case in point. The Old Greek has at this place in the text of the regnal formula the redundant verb βασιλεύει, which is present only in B a₂. The KR has the verb ἐβασίλευσεν corresponding to the Old Greek. Unless the KR were based directly upon the Old Greek it could never have the verb here because it corresponds to nothing in the MT and is superfluous in the Greek. The KR has failed here to assimilate the Old Greek to the phrasing of the MT. But curiously, the KR has characteristically substituted the aorist for the historical present of the Old Greek. This word is certain proof, then, that the KR was based directly upon the Old Greek because there is no other satisfactory explanation for the presence of the redundant verb in both Greek texts.

Verse 42

1. The KR and the MT have the name of the king that is lacking in the Old Greek. This is a unique instance in the regnal formulae of Judean kings where the name of the king occurs immediately before the phrase giving the king's age at accession to the throne and shows the dependence of the KR upon the MT.

2. The KR has the semitism υἱός corresponding to the Hebrew בֶּן־ which is lacking in the OG. Although the expression without υἱός would be good classical Greek, and is found occasionally in other OT books,[12] it is unlikely that the Old Greek preserved a stylistic variant here, because it uses the expression with υἱός for indicating age elsewhere (cf. I Kings 14: 21). The loss of υἱός in the Old Greek is probably due to disturbance of the text occasioned by the superfluous verb.

6. The KR and the MT have the copulative which is omitted by the Old Greek.

7. For the third time in this regnal formula the Old Greek has the characteristic historical present βασιλεύει as opposed to the aorist in the KR.

10. In the Old Greek section of I Kings there are three occurrences in the regnal formulae of the Hebrew expression אמו. In all three the genitive is used, as here (14: 21, 15: 2, 10): τῆς μητρὸς αὐτοῦ. In the KR section of II Kings the Hebrew word is translated nine times by the dative: τῇ μητρὶ αὐτοῦ, and only four times by the genitive.[13] It would seem that the use of the genitive in translating the Hebrew expression is a characteristic of the Old Greek, whereas the use of the dative characterizes the KR.

Verse 43

2. The KR has πάσῃ corresponding to כל in the MT, but lacking in the Old Greek.[14]

7. In Chapter I of the present study the validity of employing the different Greek translations of the Hebrew expression בעיני יהוה as a criterion for distinguishing between the Old Greek and KR was demonstrated. It was seen that ἐνώπιον was the characteristic rendering in the Old Greek, whereas ἐν ὀφθαλμοῖς was never used without exception. The KR, on the other hand, employed the expression ἐν ὀφθαλμοῖς as its characteristic, whereas ἐνώπιον occurs only as a rare exception. Applying these results to the present textual analysis, it is clear that the presence of ἐνώπιον in the regnal formula at I Kings 16: 28[b] is a strong indication that the passage in question belongs to the Old Greek text. The presence of the expression ἐν ὀφθαλμοῖς in the regnal formula at I Kings 22: 41–51 is certain proof that the passage does not belong to the Old Greek translation, but to the KR.[15]

Verse 44

2. In the other notices where this stereotyped phrase occurs,[16] the Hebrew סרו is always translated into Greek as if it were הסיר[17] with the verb in the singular, except at II Kings 12: 4, where the Hebrew is exactly rendered. The reason for the verb being in the

plural in the Old Greek seems to be that it is construed with the
two verbs that follow (see below) where the subject is the people of
Judah (understood), and not the king. The remaining manuscripts,
except for B h*i*no, have the verb in the singular. L adds the name of
Jehoshaphat.

3 to 6. This cliché occurs elsewhere in II Kings.[18] At I Kings
16: 28[b] the expression ἔτι ὁ λαὸς is absent from all texts but the
minuscule v. The rendition of 4 to 6 in the Old Greek is followed
by all the Greek manuscripts with this slight variation in L: ἐπὶ
τῶν ὑψηλῶν.

4. As was shown in Chapter I, except for the texts now under
discussion, the characteristic rendering of the Hebrew verb זבח in
the Old Greek is θύειν, and in the KR is θυσιάζειν. The presence
of the verb ἔθυον in the regnal formula of Jehoshaphat at I Kings
16: 28[b] proves that it belongs to the Old Greek, whereas the use of
ἐθυσίαζεν in the regnal formula at I Kings 22: 44 demonstrates that
the latter text belongs to the KR.

Verse 45

In the MT and the KR there is a brief statement concerning the conclusion of peace between Jehoshaphat and the king of Israel followed
by the stereotyped first part of the concluding regnal formula in
verse 46. The Old Greek, however, has a shorter text which corresponds
only to verse 45, 1–2. Moreover, the relative clause in the Old Greek
is immediately connected with the subject clause in verse 46, with
the omission of the cliché καὶ τὰ λοιπὰ, and so forth. This divergence
seems to reflect a different Hebrew *Vorlage* for the Old Greek.

Verse 46

6. This is a rare example of a phrase omitted in the KR which is
present in both the Old Greek and the MT. It may be a hexaplaric
addition in the Old Greek and in L.[19]

10 and 11. The unusual translation of the KR has no typical
significance because this formula is so stereotyped that there are
never any important differences between the renditions of this cliché
by the Old Greek and the KR elsewhere.

Verse 47

This and the following three verses are wanting in B, which means that they were not present in the KR. The text given here in brackets is taken from the critical apparatus to the Larger Cambridge Septuagint. They are attributed there to Codex Alexandrinus, supported by the Armenian and the Syrohexapla. In the Syrohexapla they are credited to Aquila and are placed under the hexaplaric asterisk. There are two items that make the attribution of these verses to Aquila virtually certain. The rendering of the Hebrew expression in the conclusion of the regnal formulae ויתר is uniform in both the Old Greek and the KR elsewhere: καὶ τὰ λοιπά. The Greek translation of the expression here, however, is the same as at I Kings 14: 19, one of the block of verses also attributed to Aquila, as noted earlier: καὶ περισσόν.

In verse 49 the Hebrew proper name אופירה with the so-called *He locale*, which is actually an old accusative with an additional demonstrative element,[20] is translated in the Greek by the proper name with the addition of the particle -δε. This usage is considered to be a characteristic of Aquila.[21] Another example occurs at II Kings 16: 9, κυρήνηνδε.[22]

Apart from the characteristics just noted the translation of Aquila and the text of the MT do not differ appreciably from the text of the Old Greek in this or the following verses.

Verse 48

1 and 2.   The place name Σύρια in the Old Greek (= ארם) is evidently due to a confusion of the Hebrew letters ר and ד in the *Vorlage* of the Old Greek text. Aquila has the correct rendition of the MT.

3.   The Old Greek has a transliteration of the Hebrew, as the translator was apparently not certain whether the word was a title or a proper name. Aquila, however, has a rendition characteristic for the KR, Aquila, and Theodotion. These versions, as Barthélemy has observed, translate all words based on the verb נצב-יצב by some form of the Greek verb στηλοῦν.[23]

Verse 50

1 to 3. The Old Greek has only the generic reference to the king of
Israel, whereas Aquila, along with the MT, identifies the king as
Ahaziah the son of Ahab. This may be another proof of the transposition of the regnal formula. Stade suggests that the king of Israel
here was not Ahaziah but Ahab.[24] This latter identification is actually
made in the manuscripts gi. In Chronicles the account of Jehoshaphat's
maritime cooperation with the king of Israel has Ahaziah as king of
Israel (II Chron. 20: 35, 37). There is a discrepancy in the two accounts,
however, for in Kings Jehoshaphat declines the offer of Ahaziah,
but in Chronicles he willingly cooperates with Ahaziah and receives
a prophetic condemnation. However these conflicting accounts are
to be explained, the Old Greek text at I Kings 16: 28[g], where the king
of Israel is anonymous, represents the oldest stage of the tradition
and presupposes a Hebrew *Vorlage* other than the MT.

Verse 51

With this verse the KR text resumes in B. In the stereotyped formula
recounting the death and obsequies of the king the Old Greek is
lacking 4 and 5. Here B is defective. In every other instance in the
Old Greek text where mention is made of the king's burial this phrase
is present: Rehoboam (14: 31), Abijah (15: 8), Asa (15: 24), Baasha
(16: 6), Omri (16: 28). In all these instances, as well as in L and a
number of other manuscripts (dfhjmnpqstuwz) at 16: 28[h], the Hebrew
expression ויקבר is translated by the Greek θάπτεται. This latter is
of course the historical present, the certain sign of an older Greek
text in Kings. The KR translation of the Hebrew expression is the
aorist ἐτάφη. The text at I Kings 22: 51 has this aorist, proving that
it belongs to the KR.

The omission of the four verses in the regnal formula of Jehoshaphat
in the KR (verses 47–50) supports the contention that the regnal
formula at I Kings 22: 41–51 was a late reworking of the regnal
formula at I Kings 16: 28[a–h] because these four verses contain
information about Jehoshaphat's activities outside the stereotyped
framework of the regnal formula. It would seem that the KR redactor
omitted these four verses containing supplementary information be-

cause he was interested only in reworking the seven verses containing the essential elements of the introductory and concluding regnal formula and then transposing them to a place in the text consonant with the Hebrew chronology. It will be argued in a later chapter that the notice concerning the absence of a king in Edom during the reign of Jehoshaphat conflicts with the chronology of the MT and the KR, and this may also be the reason these four verses were omitted by the KR redactor.

At a later stage in the development of the Greek text the hexaplaric recension brought the reworked and transposed regnal formula at I Kings 22: 41–51 into perfect conformity with the MT by inserting the missing four verses from the version of Aquila. This was necessary because the hexaplaric recension had also excised the regnal formula at 16:28[a–h], so that these four verses would not otherwise have been represented in the hexaplaric text.

The following conclusions can be drawn from the comparative textual analysis just completed:

The regnal formula of Jehoshaphat at I Kings 16: 28[a–h] presupposes a Hebrew *Vorlage* that at times varies from the MT. Its lexical and stylistic characteristics certainly identify it as belonging to the Old Greek translation present in the first twenty-one chapters of I Kings.

The regnal formula at I Kings 22: 41–51 represents a reworked version of the earlier regnal formula. Its lexical and stylistic characteristics, apart from the four verses taken from the version of Aquila, identify it as belonging to the KR. It presupposes a Hebrew *Vorlage* very close to the MT but not identical to it. This conclusion accords well with what is otherwise known of the relationship of the KR to the MT.

On the basis of the data from the synchronism in the regnal formula of Omri and the principle of the alternation of series in the ordering of the sequence of regnal formulae, the Old Greek chronology demanded that the regnal formula of Jehoshaphat follow immediately upon the regnal formula of Omri. The comparative textual analysis of the two versions of the regnal formula of Jehoshaphat has clearly established that the regnal formula at I Kings 16: 28[a–h] was original to the Old Greek text. It follows that the Old Greek chronology was already in existence when the Old Greek translation of I Kings was originally made. On the other hand, the assimilation of the Greek text to the Hebrew chronology is shown to be a later stage of development because the regnal formula of Jehoshaphat at I Kings 22: 41–51, which is in accord with the Hebrew chronology, has been demonstrated to be a reworking of the older regnal formula.

CHAPTER IV

The Reigns from Ahab to Ahaziah (J)

The doublet regnal formula of Jehoshaphat is the most convincing evidence for the existence of a distinct Old Greek chronology in the period from Omri to Jehu. Other important evidence, however, is contained in the regnal formulae of the remaining kings in this period. In the present chapter the reigns of these kings will be reviewed and the pertinent texts will be subjected to the same text-critical analysis as in the preceding chapter.

The Reign of Ahab

Because Jehoshaphat began to reign in the last year of Omri according to the Old Greek chronology, the reign of Omri's successor would begin in Jehoshaphat's second year. After the regnal formula of Jehoshaphat consequently the Old Greek text moves back to the series of Israelite kings at I Kings 16: 29 and synchronizes the beginning of Ahab's reign with the second year of Jehoshaphat. The Hebrew chronology has the introductory part of Ahab's regnal formula in the same place as the Old Greek text at I Kings 16: 29, but the coincidence is only superficial. Because in the Hebrew chronology Ahab's reign is synchronized with the thirty-eighth year of Asa, the introductory part of Ahab's regnal formula immediately follows that of his father, Omri. The Old Greek regnal formula for Ahab, moreover, begins with the synchronism first, which was shown to be the characteristic way of beginning the regnal formulae in the Old Greek section of Kings, whereas the Hebrew begins with the name of the king

before the synchronism, indicating that the Old Greek had a Hebrew
Vorlage other than the MT.

The introductory and concluding parts of Ahab's regnal formula
are separated by over five chapters of narrative material derived from
the cycle of stories about the prophet Elijah and other northern
prophets. The last of these prophetic narratives in chapter 22 of
I Kings recounts the circumstances of Ahab's death at Ramoth-gilead.
The concluding part of Ahab's regnal formula is placed after this
narrative at I Kings 22: 39–40.

According to the Old Greek chronology the regnal formula of
Ahaziah of Israel should now follow immediately for his reign continues
the series of Israelite kings whose reigns overlap with that of Jehoshaphat of Judah. But beginning with chapter 22 a shift in text form
has taken place in Codex Vaticanus, so that now B exhibits the KR,
and consequently the Hebrew chronology. Accordingly, B repeats
here the regnal formula of Jehoshaphat (I Kings 22: 41–51).

The change in text form in chapter 22 of I Kings has already been
observed by Thackeray and Barthélemy.[1] With the final verse of
chapter 21 in the Greek text of I Kings the historical present (ἔρχεται)
occurs for the last time in the B text of Kings (I Kings 21: 43).
Beginning with chapter 22 the positive criteria for identifying the KR
begin to appear. It must be observed though, that the revision was
not as complete or consistent in this chapter as in II Kings. Thus the
Greek text in the first forty verses of chapter 22 does not appear to
have been assimilated as closely to the MT as is characteristic of other
sections where the KR has been certainly identified. Moreover, several
of the lexical peculiarities of the Old Greek have not been revised in
accordance with the principles of the KR redactor.

One of the more important words which Barthélemy has discovered
for distinguishing the Old Greek from the KR is the Greek rendition
of the Hebrew אִישׁ when it has the meaning of "each," or "everyone."
The Old Greek translation is ἕκαστος and the KR has the semitism
ἀνήρ.[2]

In the first forty verses of chapter 22 אִישׁ occurs four times in the
meaning just described. In the first instance (22: 10) B has ἀνήρ as
the translation. This is certainly the sign of the KR because L here
has the characteristic translation of the Old Greek ἕκαστος. For the

two other instances of אִישׁ at 22: 17, 36a, however, B has the characteristic translation of the Old Greek ἕκαστος. In the fourth instance (22: 36b) B omits the translation of אִישׁ altogether, and L has ἕκαστος as it also did for the other three instances (22: 10, 17, 36a). The following hypothesis seems to be the simplest explanation for this partial recension of chapter 22. Originally the KR was undertaken only for II Kings. The KR redactor, however, also wished to make I Kings conform with the Hebrew chronology, but without making a complete revision of I Kings, whose text at times is widely divergent from the MT. The revision of the chronology would have involved only one major textual transposition, that of the regnal formula of Jehoshaphat. The KR redactor transposed this regnal formula from chapter 16 to chapter 22, where it belongs in the Hebrew chronology, after reworking it in accordance with the principles of his redaction. He would then have been obliged to revise the regnal formula of Ahaziah, which now followed the transposed regnal formula of Jehoshaphat. The details of this revision will be examined shortly. Thus the end of chapter 22, from verse 41 on, was revised in accordance with the Hebrew chronology and the principles of the KR. The first forty verses of the chapter were still in the Old Greek translation, however. The KR redactor then made a superficial revision of these verses.

The reason he did not go beyond chapter 22 in this revision is to be found in the order of the Old Greek text. Chapters 20 and 21 of the Old Greek text are found in reverse order in the MT. Later the relative merits of the diverse order for these two chapters in the Hebrew and Greek texts will be discussed, but for the moment it suffices to note the fact of the difference. Thus the KR redactor could not have continued his work of assimilation of the Old Greek text to the Hebrew text at his disposal without rearranging the order of the chapters in the Old Greek text. But because he was not interested in undertaking a thorough revision of I Kings, he terminated his superficial revision of that book at the point where the order of the text in the Hebrew and Greek began to diverge at the beginning of chapter 22.

Fortunately, it is still possible to see what the Greek chronology was like in chapter 22. The proto-Lucian text is substantially identical with the Old Greek, especially as regards the order of the text. The regnal formula of Ahaziah follows immediately upon that of Ahab, which is precisely the order postulated by the Old Greek chronology. With respect to the correct sequence of the regnal formulae for the reigns of Ahab and Ahaziah, L is the only surviving representative of the Old Greek chronology.[3]

The Reign of Ahaziah (I)

At I Kings 22: 52 is found the regnal formula of Ahaziah (I), following that of Ahab in the Old Greek chronology and that of Jehoshaphat in the Hebrew. In B the synchronism for Ahaziah has undergone recension, and L preserves the original synchronism corresponding to the Old Greek chronology. As in the case of the double regnal formula for Jehoshaphat, it will be instructive to make a detailed comparison of these two texts in order to determine whether textual analysis supports the reconstruction made on the basis of the chronological data in the synchronisms.

I Kings 22: 52–54

boc₂e₂	B	MT
	Verse 52	
ἐν τῷ ἐνιαυτῷ	καὶ 'Οχοζείας	אחזיהו 1
τῷ τετάρτῳ καὶ εἰκοστῷ	υἱὸς 'Αχαὰβ	בן אחאב 2
τοῦ 'Ιωσαφὰτ	ἐβασίλευσεν	מלך 3
βασιλέως 'Ιούδα	ἐπὶ 'Ισραὴλ	על ישראל 4
βασιλεύει	ἐν Σαμαρείᾳ	בשמרון 5
'Οχοζίας	ἐν ἔτει	בשנת 6
υἱὸς 'Αχαὰβ	ἑπτακαιδεκάτῳ	שבע עשרה 7
ἐπὶ 'Ισραὴλ	'Ιωσαφὰθ	ליהושפט 8
ἐν Σαμαρείᾳ	βασιλεῖ 'Ιούδα	מלך יהודה 9
	καὶ ἐβασίλευσεν	וימלך 10
	ἐν 'Ισραὴλ	על ישראל 11
δύο ἔτη	ἔτη δύο	שנתים 12
	Verse 53	
καὶ ἐποίησεν 'Οχοζίας	καὶ ἐποίησεν	ויעש 1
τὸ πονηρὸν	τὸ πονηρὸν	הרע 2

ἐνώπιον Κυρίου	ἐναντίον Κυρίου	3 בעיני יהוה
καὶ ἐπορεύθη	καὶ ἐπορεύθη	4 וילך
ἐν ὁδῷ	ἐν ὁδῷ	5 בדרך
Ἀχαάβ	τοῦ πατρὸς αὐτοῦ	6 אביו
	Ἀχαάβ	
καὶ Ἰεζάβελ	καὶ ἐν ὁδῷ Ἰεζάβελ	7 ובדרך
τῆς μητρὸς αὐτοῦ	τῆς μητρὸς αὐτοῦ	8 אמו
καὶ ἐν ταῖς ἁμαρτίαις	καὶ ἐν ταῖς ἁμαρτίαις	9 ובדרך
Ἰεροβοάμ	οἴκου Ἰεροβοάμ	10 ירבעם
υἱοῦ Ναβάτ	υἱοῦ Ναβάτ	11 בן נבט
ὃς ἐξήμαρτεν	ὃς ἐξήμαρτεν	12 אשר החטיא
τὸν Ἰσραήλ	τὸν Ἰσραήλ	13 את ישראל

Verse 54

καὶ ἐδούλευσεν	καὶ ἐδούλευσεν	1 ויעבד
τοῖς βααλείμ	τοῖς βααλείμ	2 את הבעל
καὶ προσεκύνησεν	καὶ προσεκύνησεν	3 וישתחוה
αὐτοῖς	αὐτοῖς	4 לו
καὶ παρώργισεν	καὶ παρώργισεν	5 ויכעס
	τὸν Κύριον	6 את יהוה
	θεὸν Ἰσραήλ	7 אלהי ישראל
παρὰ πάντας	κατὰ πάντα	8 ככל
τοὺς γενομένους	τὰ γενόμενα	9 אשר עשה
ἔμπροσθεν αὐτοῦ	ἔμπροσθεν αὐτοῦ	10 אביו

καὶ ἠθέτησεν Μωάβ
ἐν Ἰσραήλ
μετὰ τὸ ἀποθανεῖν
Ἀχαάβ

Verse 52

1 and 2. The same discrepancy between the Greek texts is to be noted here as in the case of the two regnal formulae for Jehoshaphat. In the structuring of the introductory part of the regnal formula L begins with the synchronism, which was seen earlier to be the more usual pattern in regnal formulae. B, in conformity with the MT, begins with the name of the king. This diversity of structure in the Greek texts presupposes diverse Hebrew *Vorlagen*.

In the phrasing of the synchronism, moreover, L has the same type of expression (Greek expression IV) as the Old Greek regnal formula for Jehoshaphat at I Kings 16: 28ᵃ. Greek expression IV was seen to be a characteristic of the Old Greek section of Kings.⁴

3. The most important criterion for distinguishing recensions in regnal formulae, as already discussed, is the translation of the Hebrew מלך. Here B employs the aorist ἐβασίλευσεν. This is certain evidence that the text is not the Old Greek, which elsewhere employs the historical present in a like context. L has the historical present βασιλεύει indicating what the usage of the Old Greek would have been here were it present.

8 and 9. In B the name of the king of Judah is in the dative, the characteristic of the KR, and L employs the genitive.

10 and 11. B and the MT have an additional phrase not found in the L, which probably was necessitated by the different word order in the text of B and the MT because they began with the name of the king rather than with the synchronism.

Verse 53

3. An important criterion for distinguishing recensions in regnal formulae is the translation of the Hebrew expression בעיני יהוה. The characteristic Old Greek translation of this expression is ἐνώπιον, which is also the translation of L in both Books of Kings and specifically in the present verse. It was established earlier that the characteristic translation of the KR is ἐν ὀφθαλμοῖς. In B, however, the translation is ἐναντίον. Elsewhere in Kings this Greek word as a translation of בעיני occurs only once (I Kings 11: 19), with reference to the Egyptian pharaoh, hence never with reference to Yahweh. By way of contrast the word ἐναντίον as a translation of בעיני, even in the phrase בעיני יהוה, is found widely in other OT books. In Chronicles ἐναντίον occurs in roughly half the instances where the Greek translates בעיני יהוה.

Because of the unusual translation ἐναντίον in B, verse 53 cannot be identified simply as the work of the KR redactor (see below).

6 and 7. These two phrases give evidence that B was probably a reworking of the Old Greek, as reflected here by L. In these two phrases B has both the elements present in L, the names of Ahab

and Jezebel, which are absent in the MT. At the same time, it has the two elements in the MT which are missing in L, the expressions אביו and ובדרך. B here is conflate. The most reasonable explanation for this is that an Old Greek text resembling L was assimilated to the MT without omitting the elements in the older text that do not correspond to anything in the MT. The hexaplaric recension was more thorough and placed these elements under the obelus.[5]

Verse 54

8 to 10. The *Vorlage* of L must have been: מכל אשר לפניו. B represents only the beginning of an assimilation to the MT with the change of the first word in the Hebrew phrase just cited from מכל to ככל. B also understood כל אשר in a different way from that of L but ends the verse in agreement with L against the MT.

The final notice concerning the revolt of Mesha of Moab found in both of the Greek texts is identical to the opening clause in the first verse of II Kings, which follows immediately. It was apparently a scribal practice to write this opening verse of the new book at the end of the preceding book.[6]

To conclude the textual analysis the following observations can be made concerning the regnal formula in B: 1. It is much closer to the MT in structure and word order than the text in L, of which the B text seems to be a reworking. 2. It has one important characteristic of the KR, the replacement of the historical present by the aorist as a translation of the Hebrew מלך in the synchronism. On the other hand, it does not have the characteristic KR translation of the Hebrew expression בעיני יהוה, ἐν ὀφθαλμοῖς, but the anomalous ἐναντίον. 3. It has the synchronism of the Hebrew chronology, whereas L has the synchronism of the Greek chronology.

Rahlfs, when he confines his remarks to criticism of the text, nearly always comes to a correct evaluation of the relative antiquity of the Greek texts under comparison, as in the present instance. He has seen that the synchronism in L for the regnal formula of Ahaziah is in accord with the Old Greek chronology.[7] But because of his radically erroneous view of the character of the Lucianic recension, Rahlfs repeatedly shies away from drawing the conclusion his textual analysis demands. He discounts the evidence of L by suggesting that

Lucian could have corrected his text back into conformity with the data of the Old Greek text.[8] It is surely sounder to conclude, at least from a methodological standpoint, that L has preserved the Old Greek chronology, than that a redactor late in the Christian period has arbitrarily corrected his text back into conformity with the Greek chronology.

The following is an attempt to reconcile the conflicting evidence in 2 above. The regnal formula of Ahaziah did not have to be transposed from elsewhere by the KR redactor, as in the case of the regnal formula of Jehoshaphat because it was already at I Kings 22: 52–54 in the Old Greek text. The essential element requiring revision was the synchronism in verse 52. This verse was revised into perfect correspondence with a text closely akin to the MT. The formula for the synchronism, having the name of the king before the synchronism, was completely different from the formula used in the Old Greek and Lucianic texts. In this same verse the KR redactor made his characteristic change of the historical present to the aorist. In verse 53, however, he failed to make the characteristic change of ἐνώπιον to ἐν ὀφθαλμοῖς in translating בעיני יהוה. In II Kings, where this change was made twenty-three times, there are still five instances where the KR redactor failed to make the alteration. It is less surprising that he failed to make the revision in verse 53 seeing that the KR revision is more superficial in chapter 22 of I Kings.

It was left for a later redactor to make the change from ἐνώπιον to ἐναντίον. For verse 53, MS N has the related Greek word ἔναντι.[9] It was conceivably from such a textual tradition that the singular translation ἐναντίον was introduced into B at a later date. The essential revision, however, must be attributed to the KR redactor, and he must also be considered responsible for having brought this regnal formula into conformity with the Hebrew chronology by his revision of the regnal formula's synchronism in verse 52.

The Reign of Jehoram (J)

The short first chapter of II Kings is devoted to the prophetic story concerning Elijah's prediction of the imminent death of Ahaziah (I). After the king dies in accord with the prophetic word, a greatly truncated form of the concluding regnal formula closes his reign (II Kings 1: 18).

At this point in the narrative the accession to the throne of Jehoram of Judah would have taken place according to the Old Greek chronology.[10] This assertion is based on the extrapolation of data from the Old Greek chronology as exhibited by both the Old Greek and Lucianic texts in I Kings. The short reign of Ahaziah spanned the end of Jehoshaphat's reign, and the beginning of his successor's reign, that is, Jehoram of Judah. Thus there should have been an alternation of the series from the king of Judah, Jehoshaphat, to the kings of Israel, Ahab and Ahaziah, then back to the king of Judah, Jehoram. There is no direct trace of the regnal formula of Jehoram, however, at this place in any of the extant Greek manuscripts. The reason for this will be given later. But there is evidence of an indirect kind, and surprisingly not only in Greek texts, but also in the MT, which is otherwise the monolithic witness to the Hebrew chronology, that Jehoram's reign followed immediately upon that of Ahaziah (I).

At II Kings 1: 18 [a–d] the Greek text has the regnal formula of Joram of Israel, corresponding to a doublet in the Greek text at II Kings 3: 1–3 where the MT has its regnal formula for Joram. This doublet will be subjected to a detailed textual analysis shortly. In L the accession year of Joram of Israel is synchronized with the second year of Jehoram of Judah, implying obviously that the latter king had himself already ascended the throne of Judah in the second year of Ahaziah of Israel. In other words L seems here to be continuing the Greek chronology despite the puzzling absence of the regnal formula of Jehoram of Judah from its expected place.

It might be objected at this juncture that the synchronism in L at II Kings 1: 18 [a] is merely a late alteration of the Greek text by the Lucianic redactor, or that the whole regnal formula at II Kings 1: 18[a–d] is a late interpolation in the Greek text in conflict with the doublet at II Kings 3: 1–3.

In reply to these objections the first step will be to determine the character of the regnal formula at II Kings 1: 18[a–d]. It was shown earlier in the case of the other double regnal formula (I Kings 16: 28[a–h] = I Kings 22: 41–51) that the first of these belonged to the Old Greek translation, and the second belonged to the KR. The same identification is now made for the doublet in II Kings. The four verses in II Kings 1: 18[a–d] are the only surviving remnants of the Old Greek translation in II Kings. The Greek text at II Kings 3: 1–3 belongs to the KR and is directly based upon a Hebrew *Vorlage* close to the MT. These assertions will now be demonstrated by a comparative textual analysis.

II Kings 1: 18 ᵃ⁻ᵈ	II Kings 3: 1–3	
Verse 18ᵃ	Verse 1	
καὶ Ἰωρὰμ	καὶ Ἰωρὰμ	ויהורם 1
υἱὸς Ἀχαὰβ	υἱὸς Ἀχαὰβ	בן אחאב 2
βασιλεύει	ἐβασίλευσεν	מלך 3
ἐπὶ Ἰσραὴλ	ἐν Ἰσραὴλ	על ישראל 4
ἐν Σαμαρείᾳ		בשמרון 5
ἔτη δέκα δύο ἐν ἔτει	ἐν ἔτει	בשנת 6
ὀκτωκαιδεκάτῳ	ὀκτωκαιδεκάτῳ	שמנה עשרה 7
Ἰωσαφὰθ	Ἰωσαφὰθ	ליהושפט 8
βασιλέως Ἰούδα	βασιλεῖ Ἰούδα	מלך יהודה 9
	καὶ ἐβασίλευσεν	וימלך 10
	δώδεκα	שתים עשרה 11
	ἔτη	שנה 12
Verse 18ᵇ	Verse 2	
καὶ ἐποίησεν	καὶ ἐποίησεν	ויעשה 1
τὸ πονηρὸν	τὸ πονηρὸν	הרע 2
ἐνώπιον Κυρίου	ἐν ὀφθαλμοῖς Κυρίου	בעיני יהוה 3
πλὴν οὐχ	πλὴν οὐχ	רק לא 4
ὡς οἱ ἀδελφοὶ αὐτοῦ	ὡς ὁ πατὴρ αὐτοῦ	כאביו 5
οὐδὲ ὡς ἡ μήτηρ αὐτοῦ	καὶ οὐχ ὡς ἡ μήτηρ αὐτοῦ	וכאמו 6
Verse 18ᶜ		
καὶ ἀπέστειλεν	καὶ μετέστησεν	ויסר 7
τὰς στήλας	τὰς στήλας	את מצבת 8
τοῦ Βάαλ	τοῦ βάαλ	הבעל 9
ἃς ἐποίησεν	ἃς ἐποίησεν	אשר עשה 10
ὁ πατὴρ αὐτοῦ	ὁ πατὴρ αὐτοῦ	אביו 11
καὶ συνέτριψεν αὐτάς		
	Verse 3	
πλὴν ἐν ταῖς ἁμαρτίαις	πλὴν ἐν τῇ ἁμαρτίᾳ	רק בחטאות 1
οἴκου Ἰεροβοὰμ	Ἰεροβοὰμ	ירבעם 2

<table>
<tr><td>ὅς ἐξήμαρτεν</td><td>υἱοῦ Ναβὰτ
ὃς ἐξήμαρτεν</td><td>בן נבט 3
אשר החטיא 4</td></tr>
</table>

ὅς ἐξήμαρτεν	υἱοῦ Ναβὰτ	בן נבט 3
τὸν Ἰσραὴλ	ὃς ἐξήμαρτεν	אשר החטיא 4
ἐκολλήθη	τὸν Ἰσραὴλ	את ישראל 5
οὐκ ἀπέστη	ἐκολλήθη	דבק 6
ἀπ' αὐτῶν	οὐκ ἀπέστη	לא סר 7
	ἀπ' αὐτῆς	ממנה 8

Verse 18ᵈ
καὶ ἐθυμώθη
ὀργῇ Κύριος
εἰς τὸν οἶκον Ἀχαὰβ

Verse 1

3. Once again, in these regnal formulae the most important word for identifying the text type to which they belong is the translation of the Hebrew verb מלך. The historical present, which earlier was shown to be the criterion of the Old Greek is found in 1: 18ᵃ, whereas at 3: 1 the aorist is employed, the characteristic of the KR.

7 and 8. In both Greek texts the synchronism is the same, the eighteenth year of Jehoshaphat, corresponding to the synchronism of the MT at 3: 1. The Old Greek text here has the synchronism of the Hebrew chronology, which at first view is disconcerting. It is obvious, however, that only two words need be changed in order to convert this synchronism into the Old Greek chronology, and vice versa: ὀκτωκαιδεκάτῳ Ἰωσαφάθ. As in the case of the regnal formula of Ahaziah (I) in I Kings, L must be consulted at this point for it has proven thus far to be the best witness to the Old Greek chronology. In verse 1: 18ᵃ, in place of the two words just cited, L has the following phrase: δευτέρῳ τοῦ Ἰωρὰμ υἱοῦ Ἰωσαφάτ. As mentioned earlier, this synchronism is in perfect accord with the Old Greek chronology projected on the basis of data contained in the earlier regnal formulae.

9. The name of the king is characteristically in the dative, the sign of the KR, whereas the Old Greek practice of employing the genitive is evidenced by the text at 1: 18ᵃ.

Verse 2

3. Another significant criterion for distinguishing the Greek texts is the translation of Hebrew בעיני יהוה. 3: 2 has the characteristic

rendition of the KR ἐν ὀφθαλμοῖς and 1:18ᵃ has the Old Greek
translation ἐνώπιον.

5. The reading of 1:18ᵃ, οἱ ἀδελφοί which differs from the reading
of 3:2 in the Greek and Hebrew, ὁ πατὴρ, presupposes a different
Hebrew *Vorlage*.

6. For the replacement of -δε by καί as a KR characteristic,
see *DA*, p. 104.

11. The reading at 1:18ᵃ καὶ συνέτριψεν αὐτάς indicates a longer
text in its Hebrew *Vorlage*.

Verse 3

2 and 3. The phrase οἴκου 'Ιεροβοὰμ indicates that the text at
1:18ᶜ had a Hebrew *Vorlage* other than the text at 3:3, which
agrees with the MT.

The additional verse at 1:18ᵈ points to an originally longer Hebrew
text at this place.

The divergences from the MT just noted for the Greek text at
1:18ᵃ⁻ᵈ show that the latter text had a Hebrew *Vorlage* other than
the MT. Moreover, characteristic rendition of certain phrases by
1:18ᵃ⁻ᵈ demonstrates that it belongs to the Old Greek translation,
and is the older of the two regnal formulae of Joram under comparison.[11]

Rahlfs once again has correctly assessed the linguistic evidence.
He has seen that the presence of ἐνώπιον in the text at 1:18ᵃ⁻ᵈ
as a translation of בעיני יהוה is proof that this text belongs to the
Old Greek translation.[12] As noted earlier, however, Rahlf's prejudice
against the Lucianic text prevents him from recognizing the antiquity
of L at 1:18ᵃ⁻ᵈ, which has the same translation of בעיני יהוה by
ἐνώπιον. Accordingly, he maintains that the Lucianic chronology
here is dependent upon the MT[13] and makes the incredible assertion
that L has retranslated the instances of ἐν ὀφθαλμοῖς as a translation
of בעיני יהוה back to ἐνώπιον in II Kings.[14]

Two questions arise with regard to these few verses of the Old
Greek at 1:18ᵃ⁻ᵈ. Why were they not completely revised by the KR
redactor? Or why, if unrevised, is the synchronism the same as in
the Hebrew chronology?

The answer to the first of these questions follows from one of the basic principles of the KR redactor in his revision of an older text into conformity with a Hebrew text very close to the MT. If a passage in the old text corresponds to nothing in the proto-Masoretic text, then there is no need for revision. The old text is left as it is but is not excised from the revised text.[15] As 1: 18 [a-d] corresponds to nothing in the developed Hebrew text, it was left unrevised by the KR redactor. However, its synchronism, which would have been the same as that still in L, was in conflict with the synchronism at 3: 1–3. In answer to the second question posed above, then, it would seem that only the synchronism at 1: 18 [a] was changed to conform to the synchronism in the later regnal formula, an alteration of several words only.

So much for the evidence in the Greek text regarding the synchronism of Jehoram of Judah. But there is also the extraordinary evidence from the MT itself. The brief text of the MT at I Kings 1: 17b will now be compared with the Lucianic text and two minuscules (x and y) representing the hexaplaric recension. The KR (= B) does not have this text.

II Kings 1: 17b

$boc_2(*)e_2$	xy	MT	
καὶ ἐβασίλευσεν	και εβασιλευσεν	וימלך	1
Ἰωρὰμ ὁ ἀδελφὸς Ὀχοζίου	Ιωραμ αδελφος αυτου	יהורם	2
ἀντ' αὐτοῦ	αντ αυτου	תחתיו	3
	εν ετει δευτερω	בשנת שתים	4
	τω Ιωραμ	ליהורם	5
	υιω Ιωσαφατ	בן יהושפט	6
	βασιλει Ιουδα	מלך יהודה	7
ὅτι οὐκ ἦν	οτι ουκ ην	כי לא היה	8
αὐτῷ υἱός	αυτω υιος	לו בן	9

Both the Greek texts under comparison are hexaplaric. The asterisk after the Lucianic manuscript c_2 shows that this passage was not in the proto-Lucianic stage of the text, but was inserted at a later date to bring the Lucianic text into partial conformity with the MT and the hexaplaric recension, here represented by the text of the two minuscules, x and y. The only important difference between the two Greek texts is that L omits the synchronism. The reason is that it had preserved this ancient variant in its original place in the Greek text at 1:18ᵃ, and it was not necessary to insert the synchronism here along with the other hexaplaric manuscripts.

It is most interesting that the KR (= B) does not have the second half of verse 17 containing the synchronism in accordance with the MT, whereas the hexaplaric manuscripts do have this addition. This can only mean that the synchronism here was inserted into the MT after the KR revision was completed. As has been observed on several occasions in the course of the present investigation, the KR was made on the basis not of the definitive MT but of a Hebrew text very close to the latter, designated as proto-Masoretic. There was still the possibility of development in the Hebrew text until the final stabilization of the text under Akiba at the time of the Second Revolt.

The present text is an example of just such a development. There must have been strong manuscript support for the ancient variant derived from the Old Greek chronology (originally Hebrew, of course) that synchronized Joram's accession with the second year of Jehoram. Despite the conflict with the other chronological data of the MT created by this insertion, the variant synchronism was adopted in the definitive fixing of the MT. It is thus a precious witness to the Old Greek chronology in a Hebrew text that elsewhere has consistently replaced the Old Greek chronology with its own. The MT evidence at 1:17b, moreover, corroborates the data of L at 1:18ᵃ and once more demonstrates that L is the best witness to the Old Greek chronology of all the extant Greek texts.

An alternative to the explanation of the conflicting synchronisms in the regnal formula of Joram as reflecting two different systems of chronology is the supposition of a coregency for Jehoram with his father, Jehoshaphat.[16] This hypothesis is based on the conviction that biblical data can usually be shown to make sense even when apparent contradictions are involved so long as they are not the result of mere scribal error. It is based also on the less acceptable premise that the data of the MT can be fitted into a harmonious chronological system.[17] It considers all the data of the Greek manuscripts to reflect late, secondary, and arbitrary attempts to improve upon the MT, whose harmonious system has been misunderstood by the later Greek scribes.[18] On such a view the conflicting data in the MT itself could only be reconciled by supposing that Jehoram had a coregency with his father, Jehoshaphat, and that the accession of Joram was synchronized with Jehoram's second year as coregent, whereas Jehoram's own accession year as sole ruler was in turn synchronized with the fifth year of Joram.[19]

This ingenious explanation will reconcile the conflicting data in the MT, of course, but can it be said to be anything more than an ad hoc contrivance to evade a contradiction to which the methodological postulates underlying this explanation inevitably lead? Leaving aside the criticism of these postulates, the following objections are directed against the assumption of a coregency for Jehoram. The greatest difficulty, and one which should be keenly felt by those who believe in the reliability of the biblical data, is that there is nowhere in any biblical text the slightest support for the existence of a coregency during the reign of Jehoshaphat.[20]

To argue that one must postulate the existence of such a coregnecy in order to reconcile the data of the MT and then that the data of the MT must be reconciled because the MT has a consistent and harmonious system of chronology and, further, to argue this reconciliation because it can be shown that all the data in the MT can be fitted into a consistent pattern, if, among other postulates, the existence of several coregencies is accepted — all these arguments are patently an example of circular reasoning and not arguments from indirect or implicit evidence in the Bible.

But even granting the existence of a coregency for Jehoram, another serious objection would militate against the acceptance of this coregency as an explanation of the conflicting data in the MT. Where else in the Bible is the reign of a king in one of the monarchies synchronized with the period of coregency of a king in the other? And even if such an unusual method of synchronization could be proved, how would such a procedure be reconciled with the regnal formula of Joram at II Kings 3: 1, where the accession of Joram is synchronized with the reign of Jehoshaphat, and not with Jehoram, the supposed coregent?[21] Is not postulating too much to say that a king of Israel had his accession year synchronized with both the officially reigning king of Judah and his coregent also, when the existence of this coregency is in itself only a methodological construct?

The only satisfactory solution to the contradiction present in the MT concerning the conflicting synchronisms for the accession of Joram is the acceptance of the fact that the MT has preserved data from two variant chronologies, the Old Greek and the Hebrew, and that these data are as mutually incompatible as the two chronologies from which they are derived.

To return to the main line of discussion relative to the position of Jehoram's reign in the two chronologies, it is evident that Jehoram's reign preceded that of Joram in the Old Greek chronology. According to the sequence of regnal formulae already studied, one might have expected that the regnal formula of Jehoram would come before that of Joram in the texts displaying the Old Greek chronology, at a place that could be indicated by the numeration II Kings 1: 18+. There is no trace, however, in any extant Greek text that the regnal formula of Jehoram was ever found in this place. All the textual traditions, including the Lucianic, which has Jehoram's accession before that of Joram, are agreed in placing the regnal formula of Jehoram at the end of chapter 8 immediately before the regnal formula of his son and successor, Ahaziah (J).

One possibility that comes to mind as a solution to the problem of the present position of the regnal formula of Jehoram in L is that the regnal formula was transposed from 1: 18+ to 8: 16 at a late date in dependence upon the KR and the hexaplaric recension. Only an analysis of the text can determine whether the regnal formula of Jehoram at II Kings 8: 16–24 was a late transposition in the text. An exhaustive analysis of this regnal formula, however, is not necessary. L does have a number of readings which differ from the KR, and some of them are clearly borrowings from the hexaplaric recension. But only two readings are important for determining the time at which L had the regnal formula of Jehoram at II Kings 8: 16–24.

The principle was earlier established, and repeatedly used in textual analysis, that the presence of the historical present was the certain criterion of the Old Greek and proto-Lucian texts, as opposed to the use of the aorist, which is the sign of the KR. In II Kings the historical present has largely disappeared even in L. Nevertheless, as noted earlier, a number of instances of the historical present have survived in L. Methodologically, it is inconceivable that these archaic historical presents could have been late interpolations in the text, so that whenever they are present in L, it is certain that the passage in question represents the proto-Lucian text and thus a stage in the development of the Greek text anterior to the KR.

In the regnal formula in L at II Kings 8: 16–24, two historical presents have been preserved.

boc_2e_2	B	MT
ἀθετεῖ oc_2; ἀθέτη be_2	ἠθέτησεν	וימשע 8:22
θάπτεται	ἐτάφη	ויקבר 8:24

The presence of these two historical presents in the regnal formula can only mean that L, and hence the proto-Lucian text, already had the regnal formula at 8: 16–24 before the KR revision was made in II Kings. It follows also that the Old Greek too had the regnal formula of Jehoram here. In short there is no reason for supposing that the regnal formula of Jehoram was ever at any other place in the text. Of course, the synchronism at 8: 16 would have been different originally. As will be demonstrated below, the synchronism for Jehoram in the Old Greek chronology was the second year of Ahaziah (I), with the number of regnal years probably as eleven. This synchronism was replaced in the late Lucianic text by the synchronism of the Hebrew chronology, which fixes the accession of Jehoram in the fifth year of Joram and gives his regnal years as eight.

At this point an obvious difficulty persents itself. How is it possible that Jehoram, who according to the Old Greek chronology came to the throne before Joram, could have his regnal formula (II Kings 8: 16–24) come after that of Joram (1: 18 $^{a-d}$ = 3: 1–3)? L provides the basis for a solution to this seeming contradiction with its chronological data for a perfectly analogous case with respect to the reigns of two other Israelite rulers in this same period of history.

After the last verse in chapter 10 of II Kings, L has a long addition peculiar to itself. Only the first verse of this addition (henceforth to be designated II Kings 10: 36+) is relevant to the present discussion:

ἐν ἔτει δευτέρῳ τῆς Γοθολίας βασιλεύει
Κύριος τὸν Ἰου υἱὸν Ναμεσσει

The presence of the historical present βασιλεύει in this synchronism attests the antiquity of this supplementary material in L.[22] No other Greek text has given a synchronism for Jehu, hence the extreme importance of this notice in L (that is, boe$_2$r; the aberrant Lucianic manuscript c$_2$ has altered the synchronism to the first year of Athaliah in accordance with its own peculiar system of chronology). Jehu is here said to have been made king in the second year of Athaliah. How does this assertion square with the other data of the biblical text? In chapter 9 of II Kings it is related that Jehu slew the king of Israel, Joram, and the king of Judah, Ahaziah, at the same time. Ahaziah was succeeded by his mother, Athaliah, who reigned instead of the legitimate heir, the infant son of Ahaziah, Jehoash, who was saved by his aunt from being murdered by Athaliah (II Kings 11: 1–2). Meanwhile, Jehu annihilated the remnants of the house of Ahab and secured the submission of the leaders of the northern kingdom resident in Samaria (II Kings 10: 5).

Because Joram and Ahaziah were slain simultaneously, it follows that Jehu and Athaliah effectively began their rule at the same time. And yet the synchronism at II Kings 10: 36 + in L says that Jehu was made king in the second year of Athaliah. The only way to reconcile these data is to suppose that Athaliah was considered to have had her accession year in the last year of her son, Ahaziah, according to the postdating method of reckoning. Jehu's first year would then have been synchronized with the first year of Athaliah calculated according to the system of postdating, presumably after the royal New Year, at which time Athaliah's official first year would have begun. According to the nonaccession-year method of reckoning, or antedating, however, this would have been Athaliah's *second* year.[23]

<pre>
                              Athaliah
              Ahaziah (ac) 1   2   3   . . .
                      (ac) 1
       Joram . . . 10 11 12 1   2   3   . . .
                               Jehu
</pre>

It must be supposed, then, that the synchronism of Jehu with the reign of Athaliah was calculated according to the nonaccession-year method of reckoning, or antedating, according to which the accession year of Athaliah would have been regarded as her first year. In this way it is possible to explain how Jehu, who began to reign at virtually the same time as Athaliah, could be said to have had his accession in Athaliah's second year.

There is yet another significant feature of this synchronism at II Kings 10: 36 +. Although Jehu's reign is officially synchronized as having begun after the beginning of the reign of Athaliah, the whole account of Jehu's activity, including his death and burial and the notice of his reign of twenty-eight years, is given before the first mention is made of Athaliah at II Kings 11: 1.

Returning now to the consideration of the regnal formula of Jehoram, it will be seen that there is a perfect analogy between the regnal formulae of Joram and Jehoram, on the one hand, and the regnal formulae of Athaliah and Jehu on the other.

If the data in L for the reigns of Jehoshaphat and Ahaziah (I) are taken into account, it is evident that Joram and Jehoram must have begun to reign at practically the same time.

<pre>
                       Jehoram
                       (ac) 1   2 . . .
        Jehoshaphat . . . 24 25
                              1   2   1   2 . . .
                       Ahaziah   Joram
</pre>

Joram's first year (= accession year), as in the case of Jehu, is reckoned according to inconsequent accession-year dating. Jehoram's accession year, the last of Jehoshaphat, is reckoned according to accession-year dating, or postdating. Joram's accession, however, is synchronized with Jehoram's reign in accordance with nonaccession-year dating, or antedating, exactly as Jehu's accession was synchronized with Athaliah's reign. As a result, Joram can be said to have begun his reign in the second year of Jehoram, even though the two kings must have begun to reign in the same year, as in the case of Athaliah and Jehu. The force of this analogy will become clearer when all the data of L for the reigns in question is put into a single diagram. The data for the the length of Jehoram's reign as well as the synchronism of Jehoram with Ahaziah (I), which is derived by extrapolation from the other data of L, is enclosed in brackets:

Athaliah
(ac) 1 2 3 . . .

Jehoram   Ahaziah (ac) 1
[(ac) 1 2 3 4 5 6 7 8 9 10 11]

Jehoshaphat . . . 24 25
1 2   1 2 3 4 5 6 7 8 9 10 11 12 1 2 3 . . .
Ahaziah   Joram   Jehu

The analogy has another aspect. Just as the treatment of Athaliah's
reign in chapter 11 followed that of Jehu in chapters 9 and 10, even
though the beginning of Jehu's reign was synchronized with the second
year of Athaliah, so the regnal formula of Jehoram (8: 16–24) follows
the introductory part of Joram's regnal formula (1: 18^{a-d} = 3: 1–3),
even though Joram's accession was synchronized with Jehoram's
second year. Thus there is no violation of the principle of the alternation of series in arranging the regnal formulae of the kings for this
period. The chronological data had to be treated in a special way
because of the unusual circumstances connected with the revolt of
Jehu and the simultaneous slaying of the kings of both Judah and
Israel.

As indicated earlier, the Old Greek and proto-Lucian texts would
have had the synchronism of Jehoram's accession as the second year
of Ahaziah (I) and the number of his regnal years probably as eleven.
One of the adjustments made in the late Lucianic revision of the proto-
Lucianic text was to replace the older synchronism with the synchronism proper to the Hebrew chronology according to which the accession
of Jehoram-is synchronized with the fifth year of Joram. As a result
of this alteration L now has a contradiction in its chronology as this
alien synchronism conflicts with the remaining chronological data of
L, which otherwise follows the Old Greek chronology perfectly.

Before concluding this discussion of the reign of Jehoram two additional observations must be made on the regnal formula at 8: 16–24.
The synchronism is unique in that it relates the accession of Jehoram
not only to the reign of the king of Israel, Joram, but to the reign of
his father, Jehoshaphat.

ἐν ἔτει πέμπτῳ τῷ Ἰωρὰμ   1 ובשנת חמש ליורם
υἱῷ Ἀχαὰβ βασιλεῖ Ἰσραὴλ   2 בן אחאב מלך ישראל

καὶ Ἰωσαφὰθ βασιλεῖ Ἰούδα   3 ויהושפט מלך יהודה

ἐβασίλευσεν Ἰωράμ   4 מלך יהורם

υἱὸς Ἰωσαφὰθ βασιλεὺς Ἰούδα   5 בן יהושפט מלך יהודה

Is this reference to Jehoshaphat in the synchronism, an unparalleled mention of the king's predecessor, support for the hypothesis of a coregency of Jehoram with Jehoshaphat? This text in the MT is one of the principal items of evidence that Thiele earlier cited for his thesis concerning the coregency of Jehoram.[24] If this mention of Jehoshaphat had occurred in the other regnal formula, belonging to the Old Greek chronology, at 1:17b in the MT, then it might be regarded as good evidence for a coregency because it is precisely that synchronism which is supposed to prove the coregency of Jehoram. On this view, Joram would have come to the throne during the second year of Jehoram as coregent.[25] Here would have been the proper place to insert a clause: "while Jehoshaphat was king of Judah." But this clause is found rather in the synchronism at II Kings 8:16 which gives the date for the beginning of Jehoram's reign as *sole ruler* according to the coregency hypothesis. This is an obvious absurdity because Jehoram evidently could not become sole ruler until after the death of his father, Jehoshaphat, at which time, under any system of reckoning, there could no longer be question of a coregency. The clause in the regnal formula at 8:16–24, which mentions Jehoshaphat as king at the accession of Jehoram, is a late interpolation into the text[26] and can scarcely be used to defend the hypothesis of a coregency. Even Thiele in the revised edition of his book on the chronology in Kings now admits that the clause in question is due to an editorial misunderstanding.[27]

The number of years for the reign of Jehoram is given at 8:17. The MT has eight, which fits the other data of the Hebrew chronology. B, which otherwise is the representative of the KR in II Kings, has the extraordinary reading here of forty years. This cannot be due to anything but inner-Greek corruption, as the figure of forty years could not possibly by reconciled with any chronological system. The Lucianic text reflects the confusion in the Greek text at this point. Two Lucianic manuscripts *b* and b′ (= b) have the number of years as eight in agreement with the MT. Three Lucianic manuscripts

oe_2c_2 have the number of years as ten. As noted earlier, MS c_2 has its own eccentric chronological system, and it is not impossible that the other two Lucianic manuscripts have followed c_2 in this reading. These divergent figures in the Greek text reflect scribal confusion but not the Old Greek chronology, which seems to require eleven years as the duration of Jehoram's reign.

Because the regnal formula of Jehoram (II Kings 8: 16–24) is the only place in the period from Omri to Jehu where L follows the Hebrew rather than the Old Greek chronology, the divergent figures for the number of regnal years in this regnal formula undoubtedly reflect an attempt to reconcile this alien chronological datum to the Old Greek chronology proper to L.

The Reign of Joram (I)

The two texts containing the doublet regnal formula of Joram have already been examined in connection with the reign of Jehoram. It was demonstrated that the first of these at 1: 18[a–d] belonged to the Old Greek translation, whereas the second at 3: 1–3, corresponding to the MT, belonged to the KR.

In the earliest stage of the development of the text, the regnal formula of Joram stood in the text at 1: 18[a–d]. Both Vaticanus and the Lucianic manuscripts are witnesses to this original position of the regnal formula of Joram. In the proto-Masoretic text, however, the regnal formula of Joram had been moved to the beginning of chapter 3 immediately before the narrative concerning the campaign against Mesha of Moab, where mention is first made of the activity of Joram.

Chapter 2 of II Kings contains several stories about the prophets Elijah and Elisha with no reference to Joram. The transposition of the regnal formula from the end of chapter 1 to the beginning of chapter 3 resulted in the anomaly that chapter 2 in the MT is now outside the framework of regnal formulae. The reason for this transposition of the regnal formula of Joram in the proto-Masoretic text will be given in the next chapter when the prophetic narratives in II Kings are discussed.

When the KR revision was made on the basis of the proto-Masoretic text, the new regnal formula for Joram was inserted in the Greek text at II Kings 3: 1–3. As the previous textual analysis has shown, this new regnal formula in the Greek was an adaptation of the older regnal formula at 1: 18ᵃ⁻ᵈ. According to his principles, the KR redactor did not excise the old regnal formula from the text. The old synchronism, however, at 1: 18ᵃ⁻ᵈ was made to conform with the new synchronism at 3: 1, the eighteenth year of Jehoshaphat.

In the late Lucianic revision of the proto-Lucian text the new regnal formula of Joram at 3: 1–3 was inserted into the text. In contrast to the KR, however, L omitted the new synchronism at 3: 1 and retained the old synchronism at 1: 18ᵃ, the second year of Jehoram. In the same way, L also omitted the synchronism in its third version of the notice of Joram's accession at 1: 17b, which was derived from the hexaplaric recension. Thus, in spite of all these late additions to L, the original synchronism for the reign of Joram has been retained at 1: 18ᵃ, a unique witness in the Greek text to the Old Greek chronology.

The Reign of Ahaziah (J)

In both the Old Greek and Hebrew chronologies the last king to come to the throne in the period from Omri to Jehu was Ahaziah of Judah. The position of his regnal formula at 8: 25–29 is perfectly suitable for both the Old Greek and Hebrew chronologies. Because it is not unusual for a king to be mentioned in the narratives concerning his contemporary in the other kingdom before his own regnal formula is given, the presence of the regnal formula of Ahaziah in chapter 8 would in no way preclude the appearance of Ahaziah in chapter 3. In the narrative describing the campaign of the kings of Israel, Judah, and Edom against Mesha of Moab as related in chapter 3, the king of Judah is identified as Ahaziah in L.

At 8: 25 the accession of Ahaziah is synchronized with the twelfth year of Joram in the MT and in B. L (be₂), however, has the eleventh year of Joram. In the supplementary synchronism for Ahaziah at 9: 29, all the major text traditions synchronize the accession of Ahaziah with the eleventh year of Joram. It would seem that the MT and the KR have also retained the synchronism of the Old Greek chronology at 9: 29 in addition to the new synchronism proper to the Hebrew chronology at 8: 25. L has consistently retained the same synchronism, that of the Old Greek chronology, in both places.

In this and the two preceding chapters the comparative chronological data in the Greek and Hebrew textual traditions were examined extensively and systematically with constant reference to critical analysis of the pertinent texts. In the course of this examination clear evidence was gathered that demonstrated the existence of two variant chronologies in the third period of Israelite history studied, the period from Omri to Jehu. An irreducible difference was found in the chronological data displayed by the MT and the KR, on the one hand, and the Old Greek and Lucianic texts on the other.

A discrepancy of some four years had its origin in the diverse understanding of the number twelve, accepted as the number of regnal years for Omri in both chronologies. The Hebrew chronology understood this number to cover the years in which Omri was struggling with his rival, Tibni, to become sole ruler over Israel, as well as the years of his undisputed rule as king. The Greek chronology understood the twelve years to include only the regnal years of Omri as sole ruler over Israel. Because both chronologies synchronized the beginning of Omri's reign with the same regnal year of his contemporary, Asa of Judah, they had to diverge by four or five years from the reign of Omri onward. This discrepancy is not reconciled until the end of the period with the double assassination of Joram and Ahaziah (J) by Jehu.

The Old Greek chronology is present in B until the end of chapter 21 of I Kings. In chapter 22 there is a change of recension in B, which commences to display the KR, and hence to follow the Hebrew chronology. L, however, continues to follow the Old Greek chronology until the end of chapter 22 of I Kings. In the first ten chapters of II Kings the Old Greek chronology is also preserved in L with the exception of the synchronism for Jehoram at II Kings 8: 16. Traces of the Old Greek chronology have been preserved, moreover, not only in L, but in the MT as well. On the basis of these data it was possible to reconstruct the Old Greek chronology in its integrity for the period from Omri to Jehu.

The following observations are the application of the methodological principles outlined in Chapter I to the conclusions regarding the two chronologies reviewed in the preceding paragraphs.

The Old Greek chronology is present in the Old Greek translation as long as the latter is extant in B, that is, until the end of chapter 21 of I Kings. Underlying the Old Greek translation was a Hebrew *Vorlage* of the Egyptian text type. Thus, the Old Greek chronology as exhibited by a Hebrew text is at least as old as the translation of the Books of Kings into Greek in the third or second century B.C. The Old Greek chronology is also present in the proto-Lucianic text. This latter text, which forms the ancient substratum of L, was based upon a Palestinian Hebrew text type toward which the Old Greek was revised. The close agreement in chronological data between the proto-Lucianic text and the Old Greek wherever the latter is extant suggest that there was no shift in chronology undertaken in the proto-Lucianic recension.

The KR has already levelled through the Hebrew chronology in both Books of Kings. Because its Hebrew *Vorlage* was a Babylonian text type very close to the MT, it would seem that the introduction of the Hebrew chronology was related to the growing ascendancy of the Babylonian text type in Palestine in the first century B.C. At all events it seems unlikely that such an important change as the shift from one chronological system to another could have taken place very late.

From the existence of different Hebrew text types and from the fact that they underlay different Greek text forms, it is not possible to argue the greater or lesser antiquity of a chronology identified with a given text type. It is now certain that the Greek text forms that have the Old Greek chronology are older than the Greek recensions that have the Hebrew chronology. From this it does not follow, however, that the Old Greek chronology *per se* was older than the Hebrew chronology, for they may both have been equally ancient variants.

But there is another line of inquiry to clarify this problem: the comparative compatibility of the two chronologies with other biblical data.

The series of regnal formulae studied in the last three chapters was abstracted from narrative materials of diverse provenience. Although these narratives do not have the same precise chronological references as the synchronisms in the regnal formulae, they do have for the most part points of contact with a definite chronological sequence. The regnal formulae for the period from Omri to Jehu are inserted into prophetic narratives comprising approximately one third of the contents of both Books of Kings. The insertion of the regnal formulae occurs at different places in these narratives in the Old Greek and Hebrew chronologies. The two chronologies are sufficiently divergent during this period that they both cannot be fitted equally well into the narrative material without contradiction. The chronology that is most compatible with the implicit chronology of these narratives must be regarded as the more ancient chronology for the regnal formulae. The demonstration will not be complete, though, until the motivation is established for the alteration of this chronology to one less compatible with the biblical data but more in accord with another *Tendenz*.

CHAPTER V

The Chronology
of the Prophetic
Narratives

The brief survey of prophetic narratives in this chapter is
not concerned with determining the original authorship of these
stories, nor the various vicissitudes they underwent before becoming
incorporated into the present compilation of the Books of Kings.[1]
The chief point of interest in the comparison of the Greek and
Hebrew texts is the relationship of these narratives to the regnal
formulae studied in the preceding chapters. In the following survey
the order of the Greek text will be followed.

The Chronological Sequence of the Narratives

Elijah and Ahab. The cluster of regnal formulae of Omri, Jehoshaphat
and Ahab in the Old Greek text at the end of chapter 16 of I Kings
is followed by the first of the stories concerning the prophet Elijah.
According to the biblical accounts, his ministry was exercised prin-
cipally during the reign of Ahab. The first three chapters (I Kings
17–19) of stories about Elijah and his dealings with Ahab and Jezebel
form a natural unit whose sequence could not be altered and hence
is the same in both the Greek and Hebrew texts. The drought predicted
by Elijah (chapter 17) leads to the contest with the prophets of Baal
(chapter 18), which in turn occasions the flight of Elijah to escape
the vengeance of Jezebel (chapter 19). These stories are concerned
solely with the northern kingdom. They show Elijah as an influential

figure in the religious and political life of Israel in the ninth century when the northern kingdom faced the threat of religious syncretism posed by the importation of the cult of the Tyrian Baal.

Chapter 20 reveals the prophet as the champion of the sacral right of the Israelite to his ancestral inheritance. The story of Naboth's vineyard is completely devoid of chronological interest. This undoubtedly explains why the Hebrew text placed this story after the narrative of the anonymous prophet, reversing the order of the Greek text. The Greek arrangement is superior, however, because it keeps all the stories about Elijah and Ahab together.[2]

Ahab and Other Prophets. The stories in chapter 21 involving Ahab and anonymous prophets are concerned with the war of Israel against Syria. They have a chronological reference to Ben-Hadad of Syria but no synchronism with the southern kingdom of Judah. Chapter 21 must precede chapter 22 because the campaign of Ahab against Ramoth-gilead, which is related in chapter 22, results in Ahab's death.

Ahab and Jehoshaphat. The first forty verses in chapter 22 relate the campaign of Ahab against the Syrians at Ramoth-gilead. For the first time in these prophetic narratives a general synchronism with Judah is given because the king of Judah, Jehoshaphat, takes part in the campaign at the invitation of Ahab. The northern provenience of the story is evident because its chief religious interest lies in the vision of Micaiah ben Imlah, whose prophecy is confirmed by the death of Ahab in battle. Nevertheless the same narrative is contained in nearly identical form in II Chronicles, very likely because of the important role of Jehoshaphat, who plays such a prominent part in II Chronicles. Save for the series of regnal formulae for the kings of Judah and a few verses recounting the slaying of Joram and Ahaziah (J), the story of Ahab's campaign against Ramoth-gilead is the only material in the whole section under discussion that is common to both Kings and Chronicles. The same stereotyped elements are present in the regnal formulae for the kings of Judah which Kings and Chronicles have in common, except that the synchronisms are lacking in Chronicles. The few verses (II Chron. 22: 7–9) recounting the assassination of Ahaziah by Jehu differ from the parallel account in Kings (II Kings 9: 27–28), and the slaying of Joram is not reported.

The encounter of Ahab and Jehoshaphat is, of course, compatible with either the Old Greek or Hebrew chronology. Because of the long reigns of Jehoshaphat (twenty-five years) and Ahab (twenty-two years) there was ample opportunity for a meeting between these two kings, either according to the Hebrew chronology in which Jehoshaphat began to reign in the fourth year of Ahab, or in the Old Greek chronology where Ahab began to reign in the second year of Jehoshaphat.

Nothing can be concluded from the fact that the pattern of the Old Greek chronology has already inserted the regnal formula of Jehoshaphat at 16: 28^{a-h} whereas the Hebrew only inserts it after the notice of Ahab's death at 22: 41–51. Elsewhere in Kings mention is made of a king during the description of his contemporary's reign before the regnal formula of that king has been given. The account of Ahab's death is followed by the regnal formula of Ahaziah (I) in the Old Greek chronology, whereas the latter regnal formula is preceded by the regnal formula of Jehoshaphat in the Hebrew. I Kings closes with the regnal formula of Ahaziah (I).

To recapitulate briefly, the prophetic narratives in the last six chapters of I Kings have no implicit chronological references that are incompatible with either the Old Greek or Hebrew chronologies. It is interesting that in the only instance in these narratives where the implicit chronology allowed any freedom in the arrangement of the order of the text, that is, in the disposition of the narrative concerning Naboth's vineyard, the Old Greek and proto-Lucian diverge from the MT (OG, L chapter 20 = MT chapter 21).

Elijah and Ahaziah (I). The story that occupies chapter 1 of II Kings has no specific chronological reference but must necessarily come at this place following the narratives about Ahab, whom Ahaziah succeeded as king of Israel, and preceding the story of Elijah's assumption in chapter 2.

The Assumption of Elijah. The stories in chapter 2 of II Kings, of which the one relating the assumption of Elijah is the most important, have no chronological reference or mention of any king. The story of Elijah's assumption, however, must be placed here in the narrative sequence, for Elijah is still active in chapter 1, where he predicts the death of Ahaziah, and in chapter 3, which relates the campaign against Moab, it is evident that Elisha has succeeded to the place of his departed master.

The Hebrew and Old Greek chronologies differ as to the place where the regnal formula of Joram is inserted in the narrative materials. The Old Greek chronology places the regnal formula of Joram at the end of chapter I (1: 18^{a-d}). The synchronism of L (the second year of Jehoram) makes it clear that Joram came to the throne at the same time, or slightly later, than Jehoram. Chapter 2, which contains the last narratives concerning Elijah in Kings, comes after this regnal formula of Joram. It follows that Elijah was still considered to be exercising his ministry after the accession to the throne of both Jehoram and Joram and that Elisha did not succeed to Elijah's prophetic authority until sometime in the reign of Jehoram. Conversely, Elisha must have been Elijah's disciple throughout the reign of Jehoshaphat.

The relationship of the reigns in Judah and Israel to the prophetic ministry of Elijah and Elisha can be indicated by the following simple diagram representing the respective reigns or ministry as a horizontal line and the end of the reign or ministry with a vertical line. In the Old Greek chronology the reign of Jehoshaphat and the ministry of Elisha do not overlap, nor does the reign of Jehoshaphat with that of Joram:

Jehoshaphat		Jehoram
Ahaziah		Joram
Elijah		Elisha

The Hebrew chronology has changed the synchronism of Joram from the second year of Jehoram to the eighteenth year of Jehoshaphat and has synchronized the accession of Jehoram with the fifth year of Joram. Aside from the problem of reconciling the contradictions in the chronological data of the MT, it is at least clear that in the Hebrew chronology the reigns of Jehoshaphat and Joram overlap, which was not the case in the Old Greek chronology. Had the regnal formula of Joram been left at 1: 18^{a-d}, even with the new synchronism of the Hebrew chronology, it would still not have followed that the reign of Jehoshaphat necessarily coincided with the ministry of Elisha. By leaving the story of Elijah's assumption in chapter 2 after the regnal formula of Joram, it would still have been possible that Elijah's assumption did not take place until after the fifth year of Joram, and consequently the first year of Jehoram, according to the Hebrew chronology. In this case the reign of Jehoshaphat would not have coincided with the ministry of Elisha.

The following diagram represents the hypothetical case of revision of the regnal formula of Joram with the synchronism of the Hebrew chronology, but without the transposition of the regnal formula from chapter 1 to chapter 3. Jehoshaphat's reign would have coincided with that of Joram but not necessarily with the ministry of Elisha:

Jehoshaphat		Jehoram
Ahaziah	Joram	
Elijah		Elisha

The only way to guarantee the coincidence of the reigns of Jehoshaphat and Joram with the ministry of Elisha was to change the synchronism of Joram's regnal formula and to transpose this revised regnal formula to a place in the text after chapter 2, because this chapter contains the narrative of the assumption of Elijah.

The following diagram represents the actual pattern of the Hebrew chronology with the change of synchronism and the transposition of the regnal formula of Joram. The reign of Jehoshaphat now necessarily coincides with the reign of Joram and the ministry of Elisha.

Jehoshaphat		Jehoram
Ahaziah		Joram
Elijah		Elisha

The textual analysis of the doublet regnal formula of Joram demonstrated that the regnal formula in the Greek text of Vaticanus at II Kings 3: 1–3 belonged to the KR and represented precisely the revision and transposition of the old regnal formula of Joram at 1: 18[a–d], as illustrated in the preceding diagram. The result has been

that chapter 2 of II Kings now stands outside of any reign in the MT
and derivative texts because chapter 2 is now found after the concluding part of the regnal formula of Ahaziah (I) and before the introductory part of the regnal formula of Joram. This anomalous position
of chapter 2 indicates the secondary chatacter of the present arrangement of the MT, as Eissfeldt has observed.[3]

The Hebrew chronology, as reflected in the MT and the KR,
made it chronologically possible that Jehoshaphat, Joram, and Elisha
could have an encounter, which was not possible in the Old Greek
chronology. The significance of this possibility will be discussed in
connection with the Moabite campaign in II Kings 3.

The Moabite Campaign. In Chapter 3 there is an encounter of
Jehoshaphat, king of Judah, Joram, king of Israel, the king of Edom,
and the prophet Elisha, according to the MT, which follows the Hebrew
chronology. These data are irreconcilable with the Old Greek chronology. They are equally incompatible with other biblical data. Chapter 3
will then be subjected to a more thorough textual analysis after the
completion of the survey of the prophetic narratives.

Elisha and Joram. The stories in chapters 4–8 have only the vaguest
chronological reference. The king of Israel who figures prominently
in the narrative is never mentioned by name, although it seems unlikely that he is anyone else but Joram.[4] No king of Judah is mentioned.
Thus there is no occasion in these chapters for conflict with either
chronology.

The Slaying of Joram and Ahaziah. (*J*) At the end of chapter 8
the regnal formula of Jehoram is given and is followed immediately
by that of Ahaziah (J). Both these regnal formulae would have been
here in the earliest stage of the text. The synchronisms, however,
and the number of regnal years differed in accordance with the variant
chronologies of the Hebrew and Old Greek. These two regnal formulae
are distinctive in that they do not follow the concluding part of the
regnal formula of Joram but come after the introductory part of
Joram's regnal formula, while Joram is still reigning. The reason for
this unusual practice is that Ahaziah is slain simultaneously with
Joram in chapter 9, and Ahaziah had to have been already introduced
into the narrative. In turn, the regnal formula of Jehoram had to be
given before that of his son and successor, Ahaziah. The period of

interest in the present inquiry is brought to a close with the narrative of the double assassination of Joram and Ahaziah by Jehu in chapter 9.

In this general survey of the prophetic narratives in the section comprising I Kings 17 to II Kings 9, only one place at which there is conflict between the data in the narrative of the MT and the Old Greek chronology has been discovered. This is the story of the campaign against Mesha of Moab in chapter 3 of II Kings.

The Moabite Campaign

For convenience of treatment chapter 3 of II Kings may be divided into the following sections.

Verses 1 to 3. These verses contain the regnal formula of Joram in accordance with the Hebrew chronology. As this regnal formula has already been discussed in several places, nothing further need be said here.

Verses 4 and 5. Verse 4 introduces Mesha, king of Moab, and supplies information concerning his annual tribute to Israel. Verse 5 repeats the brief notice already given at II Kings 1: 1, which reports the revolt of Mesha against the king of Israel. The notice at II Kings 1: 1 follows directly upon the regnal formula of Ahaziah (I), and the implication is that Mesha revolted immediately after the death of Ahab at Ramoth-gilead. The MT at II Kings 1: 1 employs the phrase אחרי מות אחאב, but does not specify more precisely the time of the revolt. In II Kings 3: 5, however, the expression in the MT is ויהי כמות אחאב. In both places the Greek has μετὰ τὸ ἀποθανεῖν ᾽Αχαάβ.

The only pertinent reference in the Mesha stele[5] seems at first sight to contradict the biblical evidence. Line 8, referring to the occupation of Mahdebah by Omri, says: "And he dwelt in it, his days and half the days of his son,[6] forty years."

וישב בה ימה וחצי ימי בנה ארבען שת

As line 7 refers to the destruction of Omri's house it is clear that the period of forty years includes the reigns of Omri, Ahab, Ahaziah, and Joram. If "his son" (בנה) in line 8 is taken to mean "grandson" or "descendant",[7] then the revolt of Mesha could be understood as having taken place under Joram,[8] and not Ahaziah.

The round number of forty years would then be a close approximation
to the period of occupátion spanning the reigns from Omri to Joram.
It would seem that the death of Ahab, a forceful king and military
leader, was the occasion that suggested the idea of revolt to Mesha.
In II Kings 3: 7 Joram of Israel, in inviting the king of Judah to join
him in the punitive expedition against the rebellious Mesha, says
explicitly that Mesha rebelled against him and not against his predecessor, Ahaziah: מלך מואב פשע בי. It is not necessary to suppose
that Mesha revolted immediately upon hearing of the death of Ahab,
so that Joram's expedition represented a great delay in attempting
to bring Mesha back to submission. The death of Ahab undoubtedly
meant the lessening of Israelite control over Moab. The situation
would have deteriorated steadily under the weak king, Ahaziah, until
finally Mesha felt himself strong enough, sometime in the reign of
Joram, to assert openly his independence of Israel. Thus the information supplied by the Mesha stele does not contradict but rather supplements the vague biblical notice that Mesha's revolt took place
sometime "after the death of Ahab". Because Joram's expedition
against Moab could have taken place any time during Joram's reign,
it remains an open question whether his ally, the king of Judah, was
Jehoram or Ahaziah. Both these kings of Judah are possible candidates
in the Old Greek chronology.

Verses 15 to 27. These verses contain no reference either to the king
of Israel or the king of Judah and thus require no special comment.

Verses 6 to 14. These verses contain all the references in chapter 3
to the kings of Israel and Judah. The texts of the Lucianic manuscripts,
the KR, and the MT are given below for comparision, followed by a
commentary. The minor variations in the different Lucianic manuscripts, largely a matter of spelling and having no bearing on the
present argumentation, are not noted here because they can be readily
consulted in the critical apparatus.

L	B	MT
	Verse 6	
Καὶ ἐξῆλθεν	Καὶ ἐξῆλθεν	1 ויצא
Ἰωράμ	ὁ βασιλεὺς	2 המלך

βασιλεὺς Ἰσραήλ	Ἰωράμ	יהורם 3
ἐκ Σαμαρείας	ἐν τῇ ἡμέρᾳ ἐκείνῃ	ביום ההוא 4
ἐν τῇ ἡμέρᾳ ἐκείνῃ	ἐκ Σαμαρείας	משמרון 5
καὶ ἐπεσκέψατο	καὶ ἐπεσκέψατο	ויפקד 6
τὸν Ἰσραήλ	τὸν Ἰσραήλ	את כל ישראל 7

Verse 7

	καὶ ἐπορεύθη	וילך 1
καὶ ἀπέστειλεν Ἰωράμ	καὶ ἐξαπέστειλεν	וישלח 2
πρὸς Ὀχοζίαν	πρὸς Ἰωσαφὰτ	אל יהושפט 3
βασιλέα Ἰούδα	βασιλέα Ἰούδα	מלך יהודה 4
λέγων	λέγων	לאמר 5
βασιλεὺς Μωὰβ	βασιλεὺς Μωὰβ	מלך מואב 6
ἠθέτησεν ἐν ἐμοί	ἠθέτησεν ἐν ἐμοί	פשע בי 7
εἰ πορεύσει μετ᾽ ἐμοῦ	εἰ πορεύσῃ μετ᾽ ἐμοῦ	התלך אתי 8
ἐπὶ Μωὰβ	εἰς Μωὰβ	אל מואב 9
εἰς πόλεμον	εἰς πόλεμον	למלחמה 10
καὶ εἶπεν Ὀχοζίας	καὶ εἶπεν	ויאמר 11
πορεύσομαι	ἀναβήσομαι	אעלה 12
καὶ εἶπεν ὡς ἄν σὺ		13
καὶ ἐγώ		
ὅμοιός σοι	ὅμοιός μοι	כמוני 14
ὅμοιος ἐμοί	ὅμοιός σοι	כמוך 15
καὶ ὡς ὁ λαός σου	ὡς ὁ λαός μου	כעמי 16
ὁ λαός μου	ὁ λαός σου	כעמך 17
καὶ ὡς οἱ ἵπποι σου	ὡς οἱ ἵπποι μου	כסוסי 18
οἱ ἵπποι μου	οἱ ἵπποι σου	כסוסיך 19

Verse 8

καὶ εἶπεν	καὶ εἶπεν	ויאמר 1
ποίᾳ ὁδῷ	ποίᾳ ὁδῷ	אי זה הדרך 2
ἀναβησόμεθα	ἀναβῶ	נעלה 3
καὶ εἶπεν Ἰωράμ	καὶ εἶπεν	ויאמר 4
ὁδὸν	ὁδὸν	דרך 5
ἐρήμου Ἀιδώμ	ἔρημον Ἐδώμ	מדבר אדום 6

Verse 9

καὶ ἀνέβη Ἰωράμ	καὶ ἐπορεύθη	וילך	1
βασιλεὺς Ἰσραήλ	ὁ βασιλεὺς Ἰσραὴλ	מלך ישראל	2
καὶ Ὀχοζίας			3
βασιλεὺς Ἰούδα	καὶ ὁ βασιλεὺς Ἰούδα	ומלך יהודה	4
καὶ ὁ βασιλεὺς Ἀιδώμ	καὶ βασιλεὺς Ἐδώμ	ומלך אדום	5
καὶ ἐπορεύοντο	καὶ ἐκύκλωσαν	ויסבו	6
κυκλοῦντες			
ὁδὸν	ὁδὸν	דרך	7
ἑπτὰ ἡμερῶν	ἑπτὰ ἡμερῶν	שבעת ימים	8
καὶ οὐκ ἦν ὕδωρ	καὶ οὐκ ἦν ὕδωρ	ולא היה מים	9
τῇ παρεμβολῇ	τῇ παρεμβολῇ	למחנה	10
καὶ τοῖς κτήνεσιν	καὶ τοῖς κτήνεσιν	ולבהמה	11
τοῖς	τοῖς	אשר	12
ἐν τοῖς ποσὶν αὐτῶν	ἐν τοῖς ποσὶν αὐτῶν	ברגליהם	13

Verse 10

καὶ εἶπεν	καὶ εἶπεν	ויאמר	1
ὁ βασιλεὺς Ἰσραήλ	βασιλεὺς Ἰσραήλ	מלך ישראל	2
Ὃ ὅτι κέκληκεν	Ὃ ὅτι κέκληκεν	אהה כי קרא	3
Κύριος	Κύριος	יהוה	4
τοὺς τρεῖς	τοὺς τρεῖς	לשלשת	5
βασιλεῖς	βασιλεῖς	המלכים	6
τούτους	παρερχομένους	האלה	7
παραδοῦναι ἡμᾶς	δοῦναι αὐτοὺς	לתת אותם	8
εἰς χεῖρας Μωάβ	ἐν χειρὶ Μωάβ	ביד מואב	9

Verse 11

καὶ εἶπεν πρὸς αὐτόν	καὶ εἶπεν	ויאמר	1
ὁ βασιλεὺς Ἰούδα	Ἰωσαφάθ	יהושפט	2
εἰ ἔστιν ἐνταῦθα	οὐκ ἔστιν ὧδε	האין פה	3
προφήτης τοῦ Κυρίου	προφήτης τοῦ Κυρίου	נביא ליהוה	4
καὶ ἐπερωτήσωμεν	καὶ ἐπιζητήσωμεν	ונדרשה	5
τὸν Κύριον	τὸν Κύριον	את יהוה	6
δι' αὐτοῦ	παρ' αὐτοῦ	מאותו	7
καὶ ἀπεκρίθη	καὶ ἀπεκρίθη	ויען	8

εἷς τῶν παίδων	εἷς τῶν παίδων	9 אחד מעבדי
τοῦ βασιλέως Ἰσραὴλ	βασιλέως Ἰσραὴλ	10 מלך ישראל
καὶ εἶπεν	καὶ εἶπεν	11 ויאמר
ἔστιν ἐνταῦθα	ὧδε Ἐλεισαῖε	12 פה אלישע
Ἐλισσαῖε		
υἱὸς Σαφάτ	υἱὸς Ἰωσαφάθ	13 בן שפט
ὃς ἐπέχεεν ὕδωρ	ὃς ἐπέχεεν ὕδωρ	14 אשר יצק מים
ἐπὶ χεῖρας Ἡλιού	ἐπὶ χεῖρας Ἡλειού	15 על ידי אליהו

Verse 12

καὶ εἶπεν	καὶ εἶπεν	1 ויאמר
ὁ βασιλεὺς Ἰούδα	Ἰωσαφάθ	2 יהושפט
ἔστιν ἐν αὐτῷ	ἔστιν αὐτῷ	3 יש אותו
ῥῆμα Κυρίου	ῥῆμα	4 דבר יהוה
καὶ κατέβη πρὸς αὐτὸν	καὶ κατέβη πρὸς αὐτὸν	5 וירדו אליו
ὁ βασιλεὺς Ἰσραὴλ	βασιλεὺς Ἰσραὴλ	6 מלך ישראל
	καὶ Ἰωσαφὰθ	7 ויהושפט
καὶ ὁ βασιλεὺς Ἰούδα	βασιλεὺς Ἰούδα	8
καὶ ὁ βασιλεὺς Ἀιδώμ	καὶ βασιλεὺς Ἐδώμ	9 ומלך אדום

Verse 13

καὶ εἶπεν Ἐλισσαῖε	καὶ εἶπεν Ἐλεισαῖε	1 ויאמר אלישע
πρὸς τὸν βασιλέα	πρὸς βασιλέα Ἰσραὴλ	2 אל מלך ישראל
Ἰσραήλ		
τί ἐμοὶ καὶ σοί	τί ἐμοί καὶ σοί	3 מה לי ולך
δεῦρο	δεῦρο	4 לך
πρὸς τοὺς προφήτας	πρὸς τοὺς προφήτας	5 אל נביאי
τοῦ πατρός σου	τοῦ πατρός σου	6 אביך
καὶ πρὸς τοὺς προφήτας		7 ואל נביאי
τῆς μητρός σου		8 אמך
καὶ εἶπεν αὐτῷ	καὶ εἶπεν αὐτῷ	9 ויאמר לו
ὁ βασιλεὺς Ἰσραήλ	ὁ βασιλεὺς Ἰσραήλ	10 מלך ישראל
μή ὅτι κέκληκεν	μή ὅτι κέκληκεν	11 אל כי קרא
Κύριος	Κύριος	12 יהוה
τοὺς τρεῖς	τοὺς τρεῖς	13 לשלשת
βασιλεῖς	βασιλεῖς	14 המלכים
τούτους		15 האלה

98 Chapter V

τοῦ παραδοῦναι αὐτοὺς	τοῦ παραδοῦναι αὐτοὺς	16 לתת אותם
εἰς χεῖρας Μωάβ	εἰς χεῖρας Μωάβ	17 ביד מואב

Verse 14

καὶ εἶπεν Ἐλισσαῖε	καὶ εἶπεν Ἐλεισαῖε	1 ויאמר אלישע
ζῇ Κύριος	ζῇ Κύριος	2 חי יהוה
τῶν δυνάμεων	τῶν δυνάμεων	3 צבאות
ᾧ παρέστην	ᾧ παρέστην	4 אשר עמדתי
ἐνώπιον αὐτοῦ	ἐνώπιον αὐτοῦ	5 לפניו
ὅτι εἰ μὴ	ὅτι εἰ μὴ	6 כי לולי
πρόσωπον	πρόσωπον	7 פני
	Ἰωσαφὰθ	8 יהושפט
βασιλέως Ἰούδα	βασιλέως Ἰούδα	9 מלך יהודה
ἐγὼ λαμβάνω	ἐγὼ λαμβάνω	10 אני נשא
εἰ ἐπέβλεψα	ἢ ἐπέβλεψα	11 אם אביט
πρὸς σὲ	πρὸς σὲ	12 אליך
ἢ εἶδόν σε	καὶ εἶδόν σε	13 ואם אראך

The Identification of the Kings in II Kings 3: 6–14

The commentary on the preceding text will not be the same detailed comparison of the two Greek texts phrase by phrase as was made earlier where the purpose was to distinguish between different text forms in the Greek. Here the object is rather to contrast the mode of identifying the kings of Israel and Judah in L, on the one hand, and the MT and B texts on the other.

Royal Anonymity in the Elisha Narratives. The narratives in which Elisha is the central figure extend from chapter 2 of II Kings, after the assumption of Elijah, to the beginning of chapter 9, where Elisha instigates the revolt of Jehu. In addition there are eight verses in chapter 13 (13: 14–21), where the dying Elisha assures victory to Joash of Israel. With the exception of a single reference to Joash by name in the latter verses, and the naming of Joram in II Kings 3: 6–14, the king of Israel is never identified in these stories.[9] Except for chapter 3 there is not even mention of the king of Judah.

The reason for this royal anonymity is that these narratives were preserved for their religious significance and not primarily as documents illustrating the political history of Israel in the ninth century, although, of course, they purport to relate events in the lives of real historical personages.[10] When these stories were incorporated into the Deuteronomic history of the monarchy the narratives had to be fitted into a chronological framework, the series of regnal formulae. Originally there were few if any specific identifications of the kings involved in these stories. The expression, "king of Israel/Judah" sufficed. Within the context of a chronological system, however, these anonymous designations were sometimes made specific by the supplying of the proper names of the kings in question. This could not have been entirely arbitrary because the name of the king is often to be determined from the circumstances, which allow no possibility of an alternative identification. Nevertheless, it is methodologically sound to regard the addition of all the proper names of the kings in the few verses where they are found as secondary.[11]

The Pattern of Distribution of Royal Proper Names. In L the expression, "king of Israel," occurs seven times.[12] In the MT (= KR in the B text unless otherwise noted) the same expression occurs six times,[13] with the expression, "the king," occurring once (6, 2). These expressions correspond in the two texts and undoubtedly are the original anonymous references to the king of Israel.

Despite the original anonymity of the text, it is clear that the king of Israel in the narrative of the campaign against Moab could only have been Joram. His predecessor, Ahaziah (I), was already dead during the ministry of Elijah. To make the king of Israel in II Kings 3 the successor of Joram, Jehu, would put the campaign against Moab too late because it would have had to be long after the reign of Athaliah, when Jehoash would have been old enough to take part in the campaign as Jehu's ally. The MT makes the identification of Joram explicit only once, the first time the expression "king of Israel" occurs in the chapter (6, 3). The expression has been shortened to "the king" in the MT, but the full form, "king of Israel," is found at this place in L. L inserts the name Joram here (6, 2) and also at 9, 1.

The identification of the king of Judah is far less obvious, and here L and the MT differ sharply. The expression, "king of Judah," occurs six times in L, and these are probably the original anonymous designations.[14] To two of these expressions L adds the name of Ahaziah (7, 3; 9, 3), leaving the other four instances unaltered. The MT, however, has added the name of Jehoshaphat to the expression "king of Judah" twice (7, 3; 14, 8), and has completely substituted the same proper name for the anonymous expression three times (11, 2; 12, 2; 12, 7), leaving the expression unaltered only once (9, 4). B deviates from the MT only once. At 12, 8, L has the anonymous expression "the king of Judah." The MT has substituted the proper name of Jehoshaphat. B, however, has a conflate reading, "Jehoshaphat, the king of Judah," which shows this text in the process of assimilation to the MT.

In three other places, independently of the anonymous expressions "king of Israel/Judah," the proper names of the two kings have been inserted in L. These instances are examples of the expansionist tendency of L to supply proper names for identification in ambiguous contexts. At 7, 2, L adds the name of Joram to the verb at the beginning of a new sentence. At 7, 11 the name of Ahaziah is inserted at the beginning of his reply to Joram's invitation, and at 8, 4 Joram's name is inserted at the beginning of his reply to the question of Ahaziah.

Apart from these characteristic Lucianic expansions, L is far more conservative in its identification of the proper names in these verses. Both L and the MT have left the expression "king of Israel" for the most part anonymous. Whereas L has identified the king of Judah twice, the MT has added the proper name of Jehoshaphat to the expression "king of Judah" twice and has substituted the proper name simply in three other instances, which is never the case in L. It seems clear that there was a determined effort on the part of the MT redactor to insist upon the identification of the originally anonymous king of Judah in this chapter.

The identification in L of Ahaziah as the king of Judah would be compatible with either the Old Greek or the Hebrew chronology because the reigns of Joram and Ahaziah overlapped for at least a year in all traditions. The identification of the king of Judah as Jehoshaphat in the MT, however, is only compatible with the Hebrew chronology, for the reigns of Joram and Jehoshaphat do not overlap in the Old Greek chronology.

It is unlikely that the insertion of proper names in either the MT or L was original. But it is still possible that these identifications could rest upon ancient traditions. The only valid test for determining which of these identifications is correct, if either, is the compatibility of these identifications with other biblical data.

The Identification of Jehoshaphat and Other Biblical Data

Jehoshaphat and Elisha. The central figure in the narrative of the campaign against Moab, as in all the stories in this section of Kings, is the prophet Elisha. His name is the only one that would have been original in this narrative stemming from northern prophetic circles.[15] Hence the other characters in this story can only be identified with reference to Elisha. From this standpoint the identification of the king of Judah as Jehoshaphat is impossible on the basis of the following biblical data.

The narrative in II Kings 3 presupposes that Elisha has succeeded to the prophetic ministry of his departed master, Elijah. The preceding chapter had recounted the assumption of Elijah (II Kings 2: 11–12) and the inheritance of his spiritual authority by Elisha (2: 15). In II Kings 3: 11 the king of Judah makes the inquiry: "Is there no prophet of the Lord here, through whom we may inquire of the Lord?" The answer is given by one of the servants of the king of Israel: "Elisha the son of Shaphat is here, who poured water on the hands of Elijah." It is clear from this response that Elijah's assumption had taken place before this encounter.

But according to II Chronicles (21: 12–15), Elijah sent a letter to Jehoram rebuking him for not having walked in the way of his father, Jehoshaphat. There are no significant variants in the Greek and Hebrew texts for these four verses:

> And a letter came to him from Elijah the prophet, saying, "Thus says the Lord, the God of David your father, 'Because you have not walked in the ways of Jehoshaphat your father, or in the ways of Asa king of Judah, but have walked in the ways of the kings of Israel, and have led Judah and the inhabitants of Jerusalem into unfaithfulness, and also you have killed your brothers, of your father's house, who were better than yourself; behold, the Lord will bring a great plague on your people, your children, your wives, and all your possessions, and you yourself will have a severe sickness with a disease of your bowels, until your bowels come out because of the disease, day by day.' "

If Elijah could send a letter to Jehoram in accordance with this tradition preserved in Chronicles, then it follows that Elijah was still the
master during the whole reign of Jehoram's predecessor, Jehoshaphat,
as well as at the beginning of Jehoram's own reign, and that Elisha
was Elijah's disciple during that same period. Or, put in other terms,
there could have been no confrontation between Jehoshaphat and
Elisha as the leading prophet in Israel because Elijah's assumption
did not take place at least until the reign of Jehoram, the successor
of Jehoshaphat.

The identification of the king of Judah in the encounter with Elisha
at II Kings 3: 14 in the MT is evidently in conflict with the data
from the passage just quoted from II Chronicles.

The reasons were given earlier why the supposition of a coregency
for Jehoram and Jehoshaphat must be rejected. But even such a hypothesis would not resolve the conflict between the MT's version of
II Kings 3 and the letter in Chronicles. In Elijah's letter Jehoram is
specifically charged with the murder of his brothers (II Chron.
21: 13). But this murder took place only after the death of Jehoshaphat,
when Jehoram as the eldest son had succeeded him on the throne
(II Chron. 21: 4).

From the data in II Chronicles it follows that the king of Judah
in the narrative in II Kings 3 could only have been either Jehoram or
Ahaziah. The identification of the king of Judah as Ahaziah in L
is at least in harmony with this other biblical information.

Doubt has been cast on the historicity of the tradition concerning
Elijah's letter to Jehoram because it is in conflict with the data of
the MT in II Kings, and has no parallel in the narrative in Kings.[16]
It is evident, however, that at least to the extent of making Elijah
and Jehoram contemporaries, the Chronicler was following the Old
Greek chronology.[17] The reason why the MT in II Kings 3 is in conflict
with the data of Chronicles concerning Elijah and Jehoram is that
the MT has altered its chronology in Kings after the composition of
Chronicles.[18]

Jehoshaphat and the King of Edom. The king of Edom is an essential
figure belonging to the original narrative in II Kings 3. The decision
of the king of Israel to attack Mesha from the southwest made it
necessary that he have the support of the king of Judah and the

compliance at least of the king of Edom. The king of Edom is mentioned twice in connection with the other two kings (II Kings 3: 9, 12) and is the object of a particular, if obscure, reference at II Kings 3: 26.[19] In all three instances he remains anonymous, as the kings of Judah and Israel were also in the original narrative.

Following are the other biblical references to the king of Edom for the historical period under discussion.

The regnal formula of Jehoshaphat (MT I Kings 22: 48 = Old Greek I Kings 16: 28[e]) asserts that there was no king in Edom during the reign of Jehoshaphat. In the MT the pertinent text is as follows:

48 ומלך אין באדום נצב המלך:

49 יהושפט עשר אניות תרשיש ללכת אופירה

לזהב ולא הלך כי נשברה אניות בעציון גבר:

The first three words in this Hebrew text clearly mean that there was no king in Edom at this time. According to the existing verse division in the MT, the next two words are taken as the conclusion of verse 48 with the meaning, "a deputy was king" (cf. RSV).[20] Stade has proposed, however, that the last two words be taken with the next verse giving the sense: "There was no king in Edom. The deputy of the king, Jehoshaphat, made a ship of Tarshish, and so forth."[21] This suggestion is quite plausible. In any event it is evident from the text that there was no independent king in Edom during the reign of Jehoshaphat. This fact is confirmed by information supplied about the reign of Jehoshaphat's successor, Jehoram.

In the regnal formula for Jehoram (II Kings 8: 20–22=II Chron. 21: 8–10), it is stated that Edom revolted from Judah in the days of Jehoram and set up a king of its own. The pertinent text is II Kings 8: 20 in the MT, with which the Greek texts are in essential agreement:

בימיו פשע אדום מתחת יד יהודה וימלכו עליהם מלך

The obvious import of these two independent data is that there was no king of Edom during the reign of Jehoshaphat. Hence the identification of the king of Judah who took part with the king of Edom in the campaign against Moab as Jehoshaphat is once more in conflict with the other biblical data. Gray, who has adopted the hypothesis of a coregency of Jehoram with Jehoshaphat in order to reconcile the

contradictions in the chronological data of the MT, is compelled to
dismiss the references to the king of Edom that conflict with this reconstruction of the evidence. Thus, with reference to the narrative
of the Moabite campaign, the mention of the king of Edom "is
strictly an inaccuracy there being no king of Edom at this time."[22]
In the context of the regnal formula of Jehoram (II Kings 8: 20) the
reference to the king of Edom in II Kings 3, which conflicts with the
statement that the Edomites revolted and made a king over themselves,
is thus explained: "We must suppose that 'the king of Edom' is an
inadvertent reference to the royal deputy (neşîb ha-melek) who held
office then in Edom (I King 22: 48)."[23]

When the textual evidence conflicts with a cherished hypothesis,
it is not sound methodology to have recourse to explanations that
postulate "inaccuracy" and "inadvertent reference." The Old Greek
chronology, which would have either Jehoram or Ahaziah as the king
of Judah in the narrative in II Kings 3, agrees perfectly with the other
biblical data concerning the king of Edom, as it did in the case of
Elisha. The conflicts with other biblical data make the identification
in the MT of the king of Judah with Jehoshaphat impossible. The
Hebrew chronology, which was devised to effect this identification,
is therefore secondary, and the Old Greek chronology, which is in
perfect accord with the other biblical data just examined, must be
judged to be original.

The Reason for the Identification of Jehoshaphat

The climactic moment in the narrative of the Moabite campaign comes
when Elisha agrees to inquire of Yahweh on behalf of the suppliant
kings after making it clear that he would not intervene for the sake
of the king of Israel (II Kings 3: 14). The MT and B insert the name
of Jehoshaphat here before the title "king of Judah," but the king
remains anonymous in L:

> As the Lord of hosts lives, whom I serve, were it not that I have
> regard for the king of Judah, I would neither look at you, nor see you.

The theological principle motivating Elisha's intervention on behalf
of the three kings would in general be quite acceptable to the Deuteronomic redactor of Kings. He has repeatedly asserted that Yahweh's

fidelity to the covenant with David is the reason why Yahweh has intervened on Judah's behalf in its troubled history.[24] This motivation was still valid even in the case of kings who had received severe condemnation from the Deuteronomic historian, as in the very pertinent case of Jehoram (II Kings 8: 18–19):

> And he walked in the way of the kings of Israel, as the house of Ahab had done, for the daughter of Ahab was his wife. And he did what was evil in the sight of the Lord. Yet the Lord would not destroy Judah, for the sake of David his servant, since he promised to give a lamp to him and to his sons forever.

Elisha's blunt statement to the king of Israel in the narrative in II Kings 3 reflects the same religious perspective.

As observed earlier, in the original narrative the kings in II Kings 3 were anonymous. At a later stage, however, different identifications of the king of Judah were made in the MT and in L. In the MT the king of Judah was identified as Jehoshaphat. Two considerations influenced this identification.

The first of these is negative. A later redactor or scribe was anxious that the anonymous king of Judah not be identified with either Jehoram or Ahaziah. From the regnal formula of Jehoram quoted above it is evident that Jehoram was hopelessly tainted with the sin of syncretism in the worship of the Tyrian Baal, as a result of his marriage to Ahab's daughter. The condemnation of Jehoram in Chronicles (II Chron. 21: 11–20) is even more severe than that in Kings. His successor, Ahaziah, the son of Athaliah, was scarcely better (II Kings 8: 27):

> He also walked in the way of the house of Ahab, and did what was evil in the sight of the Lord, as the house of Ahab had done, for he was son-in-law to the house of Ahab.

To obviate the insertion of the name of either Jehoram or Ahaziah into the account in II Kings 3 and thus avoid the offense to a pious redactor of having Elisha consent to intervene on behalf of Jehoram or Ahaziah after spurning Joram, who was hardly worse than these two, the name of Jehoshaphat was inserted into the text. Actually this was the only alternative from a chronological standpoint. Jehoshaphat's long reign of twenty-five years excluded the selection of a king earlier than he, and the fact that Ahaziah was succeeded by Athaliah and then the child, Jehoash, ruled out anyone after Ahaziah. Jehoshaphat, moreover, was entirely acceptable from the religious viewpoint. He ranks after only Josiah and Hezekiah as a worthy successor to David in the eyes of the Deuteronomic historian and the Chronicler.[25]

The positive consideration that led to the identification of Jehoshaphat was the parallel narrative to II Kings 3 in I Kings 22. The latter chapter recounts the details of a military expedition undertaken by Ahab against Ramoth-gilead. Jehoshaphat was invited to join in the campaign. His speeches on the occasion are remarkably similar to those of the king of Judah in the Moabite campaign. The following are the pertinent texts from I Kings 22 and II Kings 3 for comparison. In the latter text, of course, the name of Jehoshaphat is found only in the MT and in B, but not in L.

And he said to Jehoshaphat, "Will you go with me to battle at Ramoth-gilead?" And Jehoshaphat said to the king of Israel, "I am as you are, my people as your people, my horses as your horses." (I Kings 22: 4)

And he went and sent word to Jehoshaphat king of Judah, "The king of Moab has rebelled against me; will you go with me to battle against Moab?" And he said, "I will go; I am as you are, my people as your people, my horses as your horses." (II Kings 3: 7)

But Jehoshaphat said, "Is there not here another prophet of the Lord of whom we may inquire?" And the king of Israel said to Jehoshaphat, "There is yet one by whom we may inquire of the Lord, Micaiah the son of Imlah; but I hate him, for he never prophesies good concerning me, but evil." And Jehoshaphat said, "Let not the king say so." (I Kings 22: 7–8)

And Jehoshaphat said, "Is there no prophet of the Lord here, through whom we may inquire of the Lord?" Then one of the king of Israel's servants answered, "Elisha the son of Shaphat is here, who poured water on the hands of Elijah." And Jehoshaphat said, "The word of the Lord is with him." (II Kings 3: 11)

The scribe or redactor who first inserted the name of Jehoshaphat into the narrative in II Kings 3 was surely influenced by the parallel passages in the account of the military campaign in II Kings 22. Having made the identification of the king of Judah as Jehoshaphat, however, it must have occurred to this redactor, or a later scribe, that this identification entailed certain conflicts with the existing chronology. Since it was necessary to identify the king of Israel in II Kings 3 with Joram, Jehoshaphat could not be identified with the king of Judah without altering the existing chronology because the reigns of these two kings did not overlap in the old chronology, according to which Joram began to reign only in the second year of Jehoram. However, the adjustment was comparatively minor. If the reign of one of Joram's predecessors were to be shortened by several years, Joram's reign could be made to overlap with that of Jehoshaphat.

The necessary adjustment was actually made by reinterpreting the number of regnal years (twelve) of Omri to include the years when he was struggling with Tibni for control of Israel. In this way the number of years he reigned as sole ruler over Israel was shortened four or five years as compared with the older reckoning. When the other regnal formulae were brought into line with this adjustment, the accession year of Joram was synchronized with the eighteenth year of Jehoshaphat, making the encounter of the two kings, Jehoshaphat and Joram, possible from a chronological viewpoint.

The transformation of the text, of course, from the first identification of the king of Judah as Jehoshaphat in II Kings 3, until the full development of the new chronological system, was a gradual process. Beyond the adjustment of the synchronisms, the conflict with the other biblical data that the new (Hebrew) chronology entailed either was not noticed by later redactors, or was ignored as being too difficult to obviate by further correction.

Just as the identification of the king of Judah as Jehoshaphat in II Kings 3 may have been suggested by the parallel military campaign in I Kings 22, so the identification of the king of Judah as Ahaziah in L in II Kings 3 may have been suggested by the parallel campaign of Joram and Ahaziah against Ramoth-gilead (II Kings 8: 28).[26] It would mean that Joram and Ahaziah were involved in two major campaigns (against Moab and Syria) in a single year.

In the discussion of Ahaziah's regnal formula in the preceding
chapter it was remarked that L has the synchronism of Ahaziah's
accession in the eleventh year of Joram at both II Kings 8: 25 and
9: 29. As Joram reigned twelve years and Ahaziah's reign was co-
extensive with this last year of Joram, it is evident that Ahaziah
reigned during parts of two years of Joram. There is no way of knowing
at what precise time of the year Ahaziah came to the throne. It is
not at all impossible, however, that his reign of one year spanned
two military campaigns undertaken as the ally of Joram. The first
of these, immediately upon Ahaziah's accession, would have been
the campaign against Moab. A year later Ahaziah would have joined
Joram in the campaign against Ramoth-gilead, during which Joram
was wounded. Subsequently Joram withdrew to Jezreel where he was
visited by Ahaziah, and the two were slain together there by Jehu.
L, which has best preserved the Old Greek chronology in this section
of Kings, may also have retained an ancient tradition in identifying
the king of Judah in the Moabite campaign as Ahaziah.

CONCLUSION

In the Introduction it was stated that the purpose of the present study was to apply the new insights gained from recent research into the Greek text of the Books of Samuel to the c osely related Greek text of the Books of Kings. This investigation was intended to result in further understanding of the historical development of the Greek and Hebrew texts in these books as well as a fresh perspective on one of the most difficult problems of research in the Books of Kings, the chronology of the divided monarchy.

Chapter I was primarily concerned with the description of the major Greek textual traditions in the Books of Samuel and Kings. Previous studies carried out on the literary complex of Samuel and Kings allowed the certain identification of four principal text forms: the original Old Greek translation, and three recensions of it: proto-Lucian, the KR, and the hexaplaric recension. With the major Greek text forms thus classified in chronological sequence and the criteria for determining the characteristic features of each text clearly established, it was possible to proceed to the critical examination of the chronological data contained in the different text traditions.

For convenience of discussion the chronological data were divided into three historical periods. The first of these to be examined, the period from Jehu to the fall of Samaria, is contained entirely in II Kings. There is no systematic difference between the chronological data of the Greek texts and the MT. The absence of any ancient variant chronology in the extant texts renders it likely that the Old Greek translation, which has been lost for this section of Kings, did not disagree with the MT in its chronology for this period.

The second period, from Jeroboam to Omri, falls entirely in I Kings. Wherever the Old Greek is extant and free from obvious scribal corruption, it agrees with the proto-Lucianic recension against the MT in its chronological data.

The final period, and by far the most important, was the period from Omri to Jehu, which spans the division between I and II Kings. In I Kings the Old Greek, where extant, agrees with the proto-Lucianic text in exhibiting a chronology at sharp variance with the chronology found in the MT. In chapter 22 of I Kings and throughout II Kings, the Old Greek translation has been replaced by .he KR, which displays the Hebrew chronology, in the majority of Greek manuscripts, including Codex Vaticanus. The proto-Lucianic text continues to follow the Old Greek chronology until the end of the period with but a single exception.

From the study of these three periods it is clear that there is no distinct Lucianic chronology and rather that the Lucianic text has best preserved the Old Greek chronology. Viewed from the perspective of the historical development of the Greek text, it is now evident that the Old Greek chronology, far from being the artificial contrivance of late scribal activity, was the earliest chronology in the Greek textual tradition and was already present in the Hebrew *Vorlage* of the earliest translation of the Books of Kings.

In order to decide which of the two chronological patterns was original, the Greek or the Hebrew, recourse was had to an examination of the other biblical data containing clues to an early chronology. An investigation of the prophetic narratives in Kings into which the regnal formulae had been inserted revealed an implicit chronological sequence in the narratives in agreement with the Old Greek chronology, but at variance with the Hebrew.

The critical narrative was the account of the military campaign against Moab in chapter 3 of II Kings. The MT together with the Greek texts following the Hebrew chronology relate the encounter of four persons who could not have met on the basis of other biblical data: Joram, king of Israel, Jehoshaphat, king of Judah, the king of Edom, and the prophet Elisha. Analysis of the narrative in II Kings 3 revealed that the kings of Judah and Israel in this story, as in similar stories in the same section of Kings, were originally anonymous. The discordant identification of Jehoshaphat as the king of Judah in the narrative of the Moabite campaign was an innovation of the proto-Masoretic text. Because the Hebrew chronology alone makes this identification possible and because the identification of Jehoshaphat conflicts with the original chronology implicit in the prophetic narratives, the only sound conclusion is that the Hebrew chronology was a secondary development.

Considerations were suggested to account for the insistence of the proto-Masoretic text upon the identification of Jehoshaphat as the king of Judah in II Kings 3. It would seem that a pious redactor wished to justify Elisha's intervention on behalf of the king of Judah by identifying the latter with the religiously acceptable Jehoshaphat, whose name was inserted into the text. Because this identification conflicted with the existing chronology, however, the Hebrew chronology was devised to make the identification of Jehoshaphat plausible from a chronological viewpoint. Ultimately it was necessary to revise the synchronisms and numbers for the regnal years back to the reign of Omri in I Kings.

By the time of the KR, the revision of the chronology had been carried out consistently in the KR's Hebrew *Vorlage* for both I and II Kings. But because the KR was begun in chapter twenty-two of I Kings, traces of the Old Greek chronology remain in B in the form of unrevised synchronisms and superfluous regnal formulae. It remained for the hexaplaric recension to complete the chronological revision in the Greek text. In addition to incorporating the minor changes that the definitive MT made in the proto-Masoretic text, the hexaplaric recension brought the synchronisms of the regnal formulae in I Kings into conformity with the Hebrew chronology and excised the superfluous regnal formulae from the Greek text in both Books of Kings. The following diagram illustrates the principal alterations made in the revision just described.

	A	B	C	D	E	F	G	H	I	J
I	X	X	X		X		X		X	X
II	X	(X)	X	X	X		(X)	X	X	X
III	X		X	X	X	X		X	X	X

Key to Symbols

Stages in the Development of the Text

A Omri I Kings 16: 23–28

B Jehoshaphat (Gk) 16: 28 [a–h]   I Old Greek chronology:

C Ahab 16: 29–30   Old Greek

D Jehoshaphat (MT) 22: 41–51   Proto-Lucian

E Ahaziah (I) 22: 52–54   II Hebrew chronology: KR

F Joram (MT) II Kings 1: 17b   III Hebrew chronology:

G Joram (Gk) 1: 18 [a–d]   MT

H Joram (MT) 3: 1–3   Hexaplaric recension

I Jehoram 8: 16–24

J Ahaziah (J) 8: 25–29

This diagram gives only the relative position of the respective regnal formulae. Apart from item A the synchronisms differ in the Greek and Hebrew chronologies. For details consult the comparative table in Chapter II.

APPENDIX A

In the course of investigating the chronological data in the Books of Kings a number of new recensional characteristics have been discovered. As these new characteristics do not occur in the passages that were analyzed in detail during the examination of the chronological data in Kings, it seemed best to present this new material in a special appendix.

In the following paragraphs the number in parentheses after the Hebrew word is the number of times it occurs in Samuel and Kings. For the discrepancy between this number and the numbers for the Greek equivalents in the following tables there are two possible explanations. Either the passage in which the Hebrew word occurs has no corresponding Greek translation in B, or the Hebrew word is translated in some way other than by the two principal ways that characterize the Old Greek and the KR. The numbers in brackets following the data of B express the number of times a word appears in L.

Under each Hebrew word the first Greek word is the characteristic rendering of the Old Greek and of L. The second Greek word is the characteristic of the KR.

1. רדף (26): the verb meaning "to pursue."

	καταδιώκειν[1]	διώκειν[2]
α′	10 [11]	1 [–]
ββ′	3 [3]	– [–]
γγ′	1 [1]	– [–]
βγ′	2 [6]	6 [–]
γδ′	– [3]	3 [–]

2. שר (הצבא) (19): the phrase meaning "commander of the army."

	ἀρχιστράτηγος[3]	ἄρχων (τῆς) δυνάμεως[4]
α´	3 [3]	– [–]
ββ´	1 [3]	2 [–]*
γγ´	2 [2]	– [–]
βγ´	2 [6]	4 [–]
γδ´	– [2]	3 [1]

* For the arguments that chapter 10 of II Samuel, in which these apparent exceptions occur, should be considered a part of the KR see Appendix B.

3. חכם (27): the radical. The verb meaning "to be wise" and other parts of speech as well have characteristic translations in the respective Greek texts.

	φρον-[5]	σοφ-[6]
γγ´	12 [12]	4 [5]
βγ´	– [6]	8 [2]

4. חרש (5) and חשה (4): verbs meaning "to be silent". The KR appears to make a distinction in its translation of these two words. The practice of the Old Greek cannot be determined because the Hebrew verbs occur only in the sections corresponding to the KR. L, however, does not seem to make a distinction in its translation because it employs the same Greek verb to translate both Hebrew verbs.

חרש

	κωφεύειν[7]	σιωπᾶν[8]
α´	– [1]	– [–]
βγ´	2 [–]	– [2]
γδ´	1 [–]	– [1]

The appearance of the verb κωφεύειν in L in I Samuel 10: 27 is the result of assimilation of the older Greek text to the MT, as shown by the conflate reading in L at the end of the verse, and the beginning of 11: 1: καὶ ἐγενήθη ὡς κωφεύων. Καὶ ἐγένετο μετὰ μῆνα ἡμερῶν.

The reading καὶ ἐγενήθη ὡς κωφεύων was taken from one of the later Greek versions.

חשה

	κωφεύειν	σιωπᾶν[9]
βγ′	– [–]	– [–]
γδ′	– [–]	4 [4]

Corroborative evidence that the characteristic translation of the KR for חרש is κωφεύειν is supplied by B in the Book of Judges (16: 2; 18: 19) and the additions to the Book of Job attributed to Theodotion (13: 19; 33: 31, 33). Both these texts are considered to be representatives of the KR by Barthélemy (*DA*, p. 47). Although κωφεύειν thus seems to be restricted in the KR to the translation of חרש (as is also the case in the version of Aquila), the verb σιωπᾶν in the KR is not restricted to the translation of חשה. The comparative data for the verb חשה (= σιωπᾶν) are adduced above merely to contrast the translation practice of the KR and L.

5. עון (15): the noun meaning "guilt, crime, punishment."

	ἀδικία[10]	ἀνομία[11]
α′	5 [4]	– [–]
ββ′	1 [1]	– [–]
γγ′	1 [1]	– [–]
βγ′	1 [4]	4 [1]
γδ′	– [1]	1 [–]

6. מהר (17): the verb meaning "to hasten." The rendition in the KR of this Hebrew verb by the Greek verb ταχύνειν was subsequently followed by Aquila, as noted by Barthélemy (*DA*, p. 184). The three instances in I Samuel where L has the characteristic translation of the KR are hexaplaric additions supplied either from Theodotion or Aquila. The latter attribution is explicit in the cursive MS m for I Samuel 25: 42.

	σπεύδειν[12]	ταχύνειν[13]
α′	7 [7]	– [3]
ββ′	– [–]	– [–]
γγ′	1 [2]	– [–]
βγ′	– [2]	3 [–]
γδ′	1 [1]	1 [1]

7. הרה (8): the verb meaning "to conceive, be pregnant."

	συλλαμβάνειν[14]	ἐν γαστρὶ ἔχειν/ λαμβάνειν[15]
α′	2 [3]	– [–]
βγ′	– [2]	2 [–]
γδ′	– [1]	3 [2]

8. לא אבה (19): the negative form of the verb meaning "to wish, want."

	βούλεσθαι[16]	(ἐ)θέλειν[17]
α′	3 [3]	1 [1]
ββ′	1 [1]	1 [1]
γγ′	– [–]	1 [1]
βγ′	– [6]	8 [2]
γδ′	– [–]	3 [3]

The list of newly discovered recensional characteristics discussed above and in Chapter I does not pretend to be exhaustive. Not all the items listed are of equal frequency or importance. Their presentation, however, may serve as a stimulus to further investigation of the KR. On the basis of such preliminary studies it may be possible eventually to give a complete description of the KR for the Books of Samuel and Kings.

APPENDIX B

In studying two of the new translation characteristics that were discussed in Chapter I and Appendix A, it was observed that exceptions to the usual distribution pattern occurred in chapter 10 of II Samuel. Thus in verse 12 the Hebrew expression בעיניו, which refers to Yahweh, is rendered in B by ἐν ὀφθαλμοῖς, rather than by ἐνώπιον, the expected translation of the Old Greek. In verses 16 and 18 the phrase שׂר צבא is translated by ἄρχων δυνάμεως, the characteristic of the KR, rather than by ἀρχιστράτηγος, the usual rendition of the Old Greek. Barthélemy (*DA*, p. 79, note 1) has already noted the presence of a third characteristic of the KR in chapter 10. According to Barthélemy לקראת in Samuel and Kings is translated in the Old Greek by εἰς ἀπάντησιν, while the KR has the slightly variant expression εἰς ἀπαντήν. In II Samuel 10: 5 לקראתם in the MT is rendered by εἰς ἀπαντήν αὐτῶν, whereas L has εἰς ἀπάντησιν αὐτῶν, the usual translation of the Old Greek. These three apparent exceptions have prompted a closer scrutiny of Thackeray's division of II Samuel on the basis of translation characteristics.

It would seem that Thackeray decided more on theological grounds than text-critical evidence that his late translation (= the KR) began at II Samuel 11: 2. According to Thackeray ("The Greek Translators of the Four Books of Kings," pp. 266–267) the first translation of II Samuel (= the Old Greek) ended with 11: 1, because the translators did not wish to translate the narratives concerning David's affair with Bathsheba and his subsequent family misfortunes. I Chronicles, which had paralleled the narratives in II Samuel up to th.s point, has also omitted the less favorable stories about David beginning with his affair with Bathsheba. The following arguments, however, derived from a detailed examination of the Greek text of II Samuel

10: 1–11: 1 would tend to indicate that the KR in II Samuel began at 10: 1 rather than at 11: 2, as proposed by Thackeray. The reason for beginning the KR at 10: 1 is not yet apparent.

One of the most important translation characteristics of the KR is its elimination of the historical present. There are no historical presents in B for II Samuel 10. Cogency is added to this negative criterion by the evidence of L. In verses 6, 14, and 17 of II Samuel 10, L has nine historical presents, an extraordinarily high frequency.

Lucianic Text	B	MT
	Verse 6	
ἀποστέλλουσιν	ἀπέστειλαν	1 וישלחו
μισθοῦνται	ἐμισθώσαντο	2 וישכרו
	Verse 14	
φεύγουσιν	ἔφυγαν	3 וינסו
εἰσπορεύονται	εἰσῆλθαν	4 ויבאו
	Verse 17	
συνάγει	συνήγαγεν	5 ויאסף
διαβαίνει	διέβη	6 ויעבר
ἔρχεται	παρεγένοντο	7 ויבא
παρατάσσεται	παρετάξατο	8 ויערכו
πολεμοῦσιν	ἐπολέμησαν	9 וילחמו

Historical presents are not found uniformly throughout the Old Greek text. Usually where they do occur in the Old Greek, corresponding historical presents are found in L, although the coincidence is not perfect. In general, L tends to have fewer historical presents than the Old Greek, because L has undergone greater revision. In no other chapter of those sections of Samuel and Kings where the Old Greek is extant is there such a high concentration of historical presents in L without corresponding historical presents in B. The simplest explanation is that the historical presents originally found in II Samuel 10 have been systematically converted to aorists in accordance with the practice of the KR elsewhere.

Barthélemy (*DA*, pp. 128–136) has demonstrated that in the latter part of II Samuel readings attributed to Theodotion under the symbol θ' in the manuscripts M j z coincide with the readings of L.

Hence he argues that in this part of II Samuel Origen transcribed the KR in the fifth column of his hexaplaric text (the column usually reserved for the Old Greek) and put the Old Greek text in the sixth column (the column normally displaying the version of Theodotion). Thus the symbol θ' in this section of II Samuel is misleading, because it is attached to readings from the Old Greek and has nothing to do with Theodotion. Whether the spurious θ' readings in II Samuel belong to the Old Greek or to proto-Lucian is a question that requires careful study and cannot be gone into here. But Barthélemy is correct in seeing that the presence of these spurious θ' readings in MSS M j z is an indication that the text which Origen transcribed here in his fifth column was the text of the KR.

However, because Barthélemy has simply followed the division earlier proposed by Thackeray according to which the KR would not have begun before II Samuel 11: 2, Barthélemy has failed to discuss the spurious θ' readings that occur before II Samuel 11: 4. Yet in II Samuel 10 there are two instances of spurious θ' readings in MSS M j z that coincide with readings found only in L.

Verse 8

ἐν ἀγρῷ B
ἐν τῷ πεδίῳ L
ἐν πεδίῳ .θ' reading in M (mg) z(mg) j

Verse 16

καὶ συνήγαγεν τὴν Συρίαν τὴν ἐκ τοῦ πέραν τοῦ ποταμοῦ Χαλαμάκ B
καὶ ἐξήγαγεν τὸν Σύρον τὸν ἐν τῷ πέραν τοῦ ποταμοῦ Χαλααμα L
καὶ ἐξήγαγεν τὸν Σύρον τὸν ἐν τῷ πέραν τοῦ ποταμοῦ Χαλαμα
θ' reading in j

The presence of the spurious θ' readings in these verses means that Origen had already begun to transcribe the text of the KR in his fifth column in chapter 10 of II Samuel, while putting the Old Greek text in his sixth column, whence the attribution to Theodotion of the above-cited readings.

Although a detailed discussion is beyond the limits of the present investigation, attention is called to the presence of θ′ readings in II Samuel 1: 10, 15, 21, 23, 25 and 27, which coincide with the readings of L. Does this mean that chapter 1 of II Samuel also underwent revision?

Less specific than the reasons just given for thinking that chapter 10 of II Samuel in B belongs to the KR is the close conformity of B to the MT. Ordinarily this is a characteristic of the KR in Samuel and Kings. At the same time B diverges frequently from L in the rendition of Hebrew words even apart from the characteristic differences listed above. Elsewhere in Samuel and Kings such wide discrepancy between B and L is found only where B displays the KR.

On the basis of the above considerations the conclusion appears ineluctable that II Samuel 10: 1–11: 1, contrary to the views of both Thackeray and Barthélemy, belongs to the KR.

Notes to Introduction

1. For a concise and authoritative review of this phase of Qumran research see Frank M. Cross, Jr., *The Ancient Library of Qumran and Modern Biblical Studies*, rev. ed. (New York, 1961), pp. 168–194. This discussion treats both the archaic text and the early OT recensions. Full bibliographical references are contained in the notes.

2. See Johannes Hempel, "Ein textgeschichtlich bedeutsamer Fund," *ZAW*, 65 (1954), 296–298.

3. For a recent general study of the Old Testament in the early Church see Albert C. Sundberg, Jr., *The Old Testament of the Early Church*, Harvard Theological Studies XX (Cambridge, Mass., 1964). For the esteem in which the Septuagint was held by the early Fathers of the Church see Pierre Grelot, "Sur l'inspiration et la canonicité de la Septante," *Sciences Ecclésiastiques*, 16 (1964), 387–418. This veneration was due in no small measure to the patristic belief, deriving ultimately from the celebrated Letter of Aristeas, in the miraculous origin of the Septuagint. For recent studies of the Letter of Aristeas and its bearing on Septuagint origins see D. W. Gooding, "Aristeas and Septuagint Origins," *VT*, 13 (1963), 357–379; A. F. J. Klijn, "The Letter of Aristeas and the Greek Translation of the Pentateuch in Egypt," *New Testament Studies*, 11 (1964–65), 154–158; Sidney Jellicoe, "The Occasion and Purpose of the Letter of Aristeas: A Re-examination," *New Testament Studies*, 13 (1965–66), 144–150.

That Origen himself retained the greatest reverence for the Septuagint is clear from the explanation he gave of his text-critical method in his letter to Africanus (J. P. Migne, *Patrologiae cursus completus, series Graeca*, vol. XI, cols. 47–86).

4. Lagarde sketched the somewhat optimistic program for this reconstruction in *Ankündigung einer neuen Ausgabe der griechischen Übersetzung des alten Testaments* (Göttingen, 1882), pp. 29–30.

5. Alfred Rahlfs has given a brief history of the discovery of the first manuscripts belonging to the Lucianic recension in *Lucians Rezension der Königsbücher*, Septuaginta Studien, III (Göttingen, 1911), p. 80, n. 1. In this same work Rahlfs identifies additional Lucianic manuscripts. For a summary statement of the principles used in determining the Lucianic text and a listing of the manuscripts in which it has been identified see Heinrich Dörrie, "Zur Geschichte der Septuaginta im Jahrhundert Konstantins," *ZNW*, 39 (1940), 97–105. The manuscripts that have been identified as Lucianic in the volumes of the Göttingen Septuagint thus far published are conveniently listed by Bruce Metzger in *Chapters in the History of New Testament Textual Criticism* (Leiden, 1963), pp. 12–14.

6. The principal works in which Kahle develops this view are: "Untersuchungen zur Geschichte des Pentateuchtextes," *Theologische Studien und Kritiken*, 88 (1915), 399–439; "Die Septuaginta: Principielle Erwägungen," *Festschrift Otto Eissfeldt* (Halle, 1947), pp. 161–180; *The Cairo Geniza*, 2nd ed. (Oxford, 1959). For a recent summary and critique of Kahle's position by a member of the Lagardian School see J. W. Wevers, "Proto-Septuagint Studies," *The Seed of Wisdom*. Essays in Honour of T. J. Meek, ed. W. S. McCullough (Toronto, 1964), pp. 62–73.

7. Several studies by Gehman and his pupil Wevers in this vein have to do precisely with the Books of Samuel and Kings: Henry S. Gehman, "Exegetical Methods Employed by the Greek Translator of 1 Samuel," *JAOS*, 70 (1950), 292–296; John Wevers, "Exegetical Principles Underlying the Greek Text of 2 Sam 11: 2–1 Kings 2: 11," *Catholic Biblical Quarterly*, 15 (1953), 30–45; "Exegetical Principles Underlying the Septuagint Text of 1 Kings 2: 12–21: 43," *Oudtestamentische Studiën*, 8 (1950), 300–322; "Principles of Interpretation Guiding the Fourth Translator of the Book of Kingdoms," *Catholic Biblical Quarterly* 14 (1952), 40–56.

8. Cf. Harry M. Orlinsky, "The Textual Critisicm of the Old Testament," *The Bible and the Ancient Near East*, ed. G. E. Wright (New York, 1961), p. 121; Cross, *Ancient Library*, p. 175; Dominique Barthélemy, *Les Devanciers d'Aquila* (Leiden, 1963) p. 272 (henceforth abbreviated as *DA*).

9. Cross, *Ancient Library*, pp. 180–181.

10. For the change of attitude in research on the Books of Samuel and Kings already occasioned by the discoveries in Cave IV at Qumran see the remarks of D. W. Gooding, "Ahab According to the Septuagint," *ZAW*, 76 (1964), 269.

11. "A New Qumran Biblical Fragment Related to the Original Hebrew Underlying the Septuagint," *BASOR*, 132 (1953), 15–26; "The Oldest Manuscripts from Qumran," *JBL* 74 (1955), 147–172.

12. *Ancient Library*, pp. 188–194; "The History of the Biblical Text in the Light of the Discoveries in the Judean Desert," *HTR*, 57 (1964), 281–299. "The Contribution of the Qumran Discoveries to the Study of the Biblical Text," *Israel Exploration Journal*, 16 (1966), 81–95.

13. *DA*, pp. 46–47; 126–143.

14. For the official publication of two of the Qumran manuscripts for Kings, see M. Baillet, J. T. Milik, R. de Vaux, *Discoveries in the Judean Desert of Jordan*, III, *Les "Petites Grottes" de Qumran* (Oxford, 1962). The first manuscript is represented by three fragments of chapter 1 (verses 1, 16–17, 27–37) of I Kings written on leather from Cave V. The following is Milik's evaluation of these fragments: "Le peu de texte conservé n'est pas significatif du point de vue recensionnel; le TM et la LXX y sont à peu près identiques" (p. 172). It should be observed, however, that the Lucianic manuscripts for the text of I Kings 1 have a number of readings divergent from the MT and the majority of Greek manuscripts including Codex Vaticanus, which here displays the text of a late recension (see the discussion in Chapter I of the present study). The column of text reconstructed

from the fragments is preceded by a large blank on the leather which Milik calls a "page de garde." This would seem to indicate that the text of the fragments follows the division of the Books of Samuel and Kings as found in the MT. In the Lucianic text, however, I Kings 1: 1–2: 11 (according to the numeration of the MT) was considered a part of II Samuel (= Second Kingdoms in the Greek), whereas I Kings (= Third Kingdoms in the Greek) began only with I Kings 2: 12. Presumably the Hebrew *Vorlage* of the proto-Lucianic recension (see Chapter I of the present study) would not have had a major division between II Sam. 24: 25 and I Kings 1: 1, as appears to be the case in the text of the fragments from Cave V.

The second manuscript is represented by over ninety small fragments of papyrus from both Books of Kings found in Cave VI and discussed by Baillet (pp. 107–112). Fewer than a score of these fragments have been identified and used in reconstructing a coherent text. The script is dated by Baillet to the second half of the second century B.C., and the text is characterized as follows: "Le texte est parfois plus court que le TM et se rapproche par endroits de la LXX et de la Vulgate. On relève des graphies pleines." In the readings where the fragments seem to follow the Greek manuscripts, which the editor treats *in globo* under the siglum LXX, the Lucianic manuscripts agree with the readings of the fragments in contrast to the relationship of the Lucianic manuscripts to the readings in the fragments from Cave V discussed above. One reading is especially important in this regard. Fragment 11 together with fragment 72 yields the virtually certain reading משואם in verse 8 of II Kings 7. This reading is, in Baillet's words, "probablement une graphie aberrante de מַשָּׂאָם attesté par 3 minuscules de LXX (ἄρσιν αὐτῶν). TM, LXX (le mot manque dans l'Alexandrinus), Syr, Vulg et Targ ont מְמָּם" (p. 109). The reading in question is attested by four, not three, minuscules all belonging to the Lucianic text form: b (= *b*+b′) c₂e₂. The only other Greek manuscript to give evidence at least partially for this reading is g, which has the conflate reading ἐκεῖθεν ἄρσιν, conflation being a characteristic trait of this manuscript in Kings. The reading משואם of the fragments could possibly reflect the variant form of the Hebrew word מַשָּׂא (cf. II Chron. 19: 7). This reading together with the other Lucianic readings in the manuscript represented by these fragments would seem to indicate that this or a related text form was the Hebrew *Vorlage* underlying the proto-Lucianic recension.

In Cave IV, a third manuscript of Kings was found. Frank M. Cross, Jr., who is responsible for its official publication, has kindly permitted me to examine a photograph of the fragments. They allow the reconstruction of two columns written on leather, with the text of chapters 7 and 8 of I Kings. A detailed analysis of this text must await the official publication of the fragments, but it does not appear that the readings of this fragmentary text will appreciably affect the conclusions of the present study.

15. *DA*, p. 127.

16. H. St. J. Thackeray in "The Greek Translators of the Four Books of Kings," *Journal of Theological Studies*, 8 (1907), 262–278 was the first to call attention to

the intimate relation between the Greek text of the Books of Samuel and that of Kings. His thesis was further refined in *The Septuagint and Jewish Worship* (London, 1923), pp. 16–28.

17. *Die Chronologie der Könige von Israel und Juda*, Beiträge zur historischen Theologie, 3 (Tübingen, 1929), pp. 212–213.

18. *Ibid.*, p. 214.

19. *The Mysterious Numbers of the Hebrew Kings* (Chicago, 1951), pp. 167–203.

20. *Ibid.*, p. 202.

21. *The Mysterious Numbers of the Hebrew Kings*, rev. ed. (Grand Rapids, Michigan, 1965).

22. *Ibid.*, pp. 197–199.

23. *Ibid.*, p. 198.

24. "Source Study and the Biblical Text," *The American Journal of Semitic Languages and Literatures*, 30 (1913), 1–2. Many useful insights on the Books of Kings are also to be found in Olmstead's article. "The Earliest Book of Kings," *The American Journal of Semitic Languages and Literatures*, 31 (1915), 169–214.

Notes to Chapter I

1. Begrich (*Die Chronologie*, pp. 172–173) has taken data from the Greek manuscripts without regard for the text form that they represent and has combined such data with other chronological data from the MT, the Peshitta, and Josephus. From this mass of material he has reconstructed no fewer than five distinct chronological systems, which he maintains originally existed in the form of chronicles, that were used as the basic sources of the canonical Books of Kings. In the process of editing these books the five systems that Begrich postulates would have been used eclectically by the redactors of the MT and the other versions. This highly artificial reconstruction by Begrich manifestly has nothing to contribute to an understanding of the historical development of the Greek text.

2. The term "Old Greek" is used for the original translation into Greek of Samuel and Kings, in preference to the term "Septuagint," which is often used loosely to designate the entire Greek version.

3. This term refers to the first major recension of the Old Greek translation. Subsequently this recension served as the basis for the late Lucianic text. The term proto-Lucian is employed because the early recension is preserved *in extenso* only in the late Lucianic text.

4. Barthélemy characterizes as a "recension" (*DA*, p. 91) the Greek texts that he has elsewhere designated as the "groupe καίγε." This descriptive term of Barthélemy is based upon the characteristic rendition of the Hebrew word גם by the Greek expression καίγε. Barthélemy's designation for this recension will

be used in the present study and, for convenience, "καίγε recension" will be abbreviated as KR.

5. For Origen's text-critical methodology, with special reference to the text of Samuel, see Bo Johnson, *Die Hexaplarische Rezension des 1. Samuelbuches der Septuaginta*, Studia Theologica Lundensia, 22 (Lund, 1963), p. 7.

6. Throughout this study the expression "Masoretic Text" (MT) is to be understood as referring to the consonantal text that served as the basis for the work of the Masoretes. This consonantal text was stabilized during the second century after Christ.

7. See Wevers, "Proto-Septuagint Studies," p. 61.

8. Barthélemy (*DA*, p. 91) lists the principles for establishing that a given text is a recension of an older text form and not an independent translation; he illustrates these principles by a comparative study of the Greek texts in II Samuel.

9. Barthélemy (*DA*, pp. 81–88) argues that the translation technique of Aquila was an outgrowth and continuation of the principles underlying the KR.

10. See note 16, above.

11. *Die Infinitive in der Septuaginta*, Annales Academiae Scientiarum Fennicae Ser. B, vol. 132,[1] (Helsinki, 1965), p. 172.

12. *DA*, pp. 46–47.

13. "The Contribution of the Qumran Discoveries to the Study of the Biblical Text," pp. 81–95, especially pp. 86–91.

14. M. Goshen-Gottstein considers the elaboration of a theory of local texts to be "somewhat premature." His differences with Cross, however, appear to be mainly a matter of terminology. See *The Book of Isaiah: Sample Edition with Introduction*. The Hebrew University Bible Project, Jerusalem, 1965, p. 14, and particularly note 15.

15. Cross, "Contribution of the Qumran Discoveries," p. 87.

16. See Soisalon-Soininen, *Der Charakter der asterisierten Zusätze in der Septuaginta*, pp. 18–19.

17. No satisfactory study has been made for all four Books of Samuel and Kings of the Greek manuscripts and other versions that belong to the same family as B. A classification for Samuel and Kings was made by Martin Rehm. *Textkritische Untersuchungen zu den Parallelstellen der Samuel-Königsbücher und der Chronik*, (Münster, 1937), p. 14. For I Samuel see Johnson, *Die Hexaplarische Rezension*, p. 54. A grouping of manuscripts by text families for both Books of Kings can be found in Wevers, "A Study in the Hebrew Variants in the Books of Kings," *ZAW*, 61 (1945–1948), 43–76.

18. Wevers, from a study of Josephus, the Old Latin version, and the Peshitta, has concluded that there existed an early Lucianic text form: "There was thus a Lucianic text before Lucian. There is to my mind no doubt that the Antiochian text was an early revision of the Septuagint text. That it was a revision rather than a separate translation can be demonstrated from a careful study of the Lucianic text. No two separate translations could have made the same peculiar mis-translations in so many places" ("Proto-Septuagint Studies," p. 69).

19. In a continuation of the citation in the previous note Wevers has drawn the proper conclusion concerning the late Lucianic recension: "My own belief, though I have not yet been able to test the proposition, is that the Lucianic revision *circa* A.D. 310 consisted primarily of the addition of the Origenian plusses to the Antiochian text. It is a fact that the best Lucianic manuscripts do have asterisked passages."

20. The traditional notices concerning Lucian's life and activity, together with a good summary presentation of the evidence (apart from the recent manuscript finds in the Judean desert) for the existence of a proto-Lucian text form, are given by Bruce M. Metzger in the first chapter ("The Lucianic Recension of the Greek Bible") of his *Chapters in the History of New Testament Textual Criticism* (Leiden, 1963), pp. 1–41.

21. The objection, however, that the stylistic characteristics generally attributed to Lucian may have been already present in the earlier Greek text is made by Bonifatius Fischer in "Lukian-Lesarten in der Vetus Latina der vier Königsbücher," *Miscellanea Biblica et Orientalia R. P. Athanasio Miller O. S. B. Oblata* (Rome, 1951), 175–176.

22. "A New Qumran Biblical Fragment Related to the Original Hebrew Underlying the Septuagint," *BASOR*, 132 (1953), 15–26; "The Oldest Manuscripts from Qumran," *JBL*, 74 (1955), 142–172.

23. "The History of the Biblical Text in the Light of the Discoveries in the Judean desert," *HTR*, 57 (1964), 281–299.

24. *Ancient Library*, pp. 188–190.

25. The Old Palestinian text was also used by the Chronicler. Cross has adduced the agreement of the manuscripts of Samuel from Qumran with readings in Chronicles as further evidence for the Palestinian *Vorlage* of the proto-Lucian recension ("History of the Biblical Text," pp. 294–295).

26. An earlier study of the Greek Minor Prophets scroll was published by Barthélemy in "Redécouverte d'un chaînon manquant de l'histoire de la septante," *RB*, 60 (1953), 18–29.

27. Less than half his recent book, *Les Devanciers d'Aquila*, is devoted to the analysis of the Minor Prophets text. The remainder of the work is concerned with a number of problems connected with the history of the development of the Greek text.

28. *DA*, pp. 126–127.

29. *Ibid.*, p. 127.

30. *Ibid.*

31. *Ibid.*, pp. 92–125.

32. In addition to the criticism made by Cross of Barthélemy's views on the character of the Lucianic text ("History of the Biblical Text," p. 295), see also Sidney Jellicoe's review of *Les Devanciers d'Aquila* in *JAOS*, 84 (1964), 179.

33. The close affinity of the Old Greek and proto-Lucian is due ultimately to the common derivation of their Hebrew *Vorlagen* from an Old Palestinian Hebrew text form.

34. The comparative material of the Greek and Hebrew texts has been conveniently arranged in parallel columns in Henry Swete's *An Introduction to the Old Testament in Greek*, 2nd ed. (Cambridge, Eng., 1914), p. 232.

35. See Thackeray's classification of the various books of the Septuagint from the standpoint of Greek style in *A Grammar of the Old Testament in Greek*, I (Cambridge, Eng., 1909), pp. 6–16.

36. "The first stage then in the history of the Greek recensions was the proto-Lucian recension of the second or first century B.C., revised to conform to a Palestinian Hebrew text" (Cross, "History of the Biblical Text," pp. 295–296).

37. "This Old Greek text was revised no later than the first century B.C. toward a Hebrew text we can trace in Palestine in the Chronicles and in the three manuscripts from Cave IV, Qumran. The Greek form is extant in quotations in Josephus, in the substratum of the Lucianic recension preserved in the Greek minuscules boc_2e_2, and surprisingly enough, in the sixth column of Origen's Hexapla to II Samuel 11: 2–I Kings 2: 11" (*ibid.*, p. 295).

38. The number in parentheses which follows the symbol is that assigned to the manuscript by Rahlfs: b = b′ (19) + b (108); o (82); e_2 (93); c_2 (127).

39. An excellent witness also to the Lucianic text is MS r, which is extant for the following parts of II Kings: 1: 19–4: 31, 10: 3–11: 15; 12: 4–17: 37; 18: 9–19: 24. For the sub-Lucianic manuscripts in I Samuel see Johnson, *Die Hexaplarische Rezension*, p. 20. A listing of these manuscripts for all four Books of Samuel and Kings is also given by Primus Vannutelli, *Libri synoptici Veteris Testamenti seu librorum Regnum et Chronicorum loci paralleli* (Rome, 1931), p. vi.

40. *DA*, pp. 144–157.

41. *Ibid.*, pp. 128–136.

42. *Ibid.*, p. 143.

43. *Ibid.*, pp. 102–110.

44. Barthélemy argues that this concern was prompted by the exigencies of a school of Palestinian rabbinical exegesis that flourished before Rabbi Akiba (*DA*, p. 31).

45. These can be found arranged in tabular form in Thackeray, *The Septuagint and Jewish Worship*, (London, 1923), pp. 114–115.

46. The new criteria proposed by Barthélemy are discussed in *DA*, pp. 48–54, 59–60, 65–68, 78–80. For less significant criteria see also pp. 81–88; 102–109; 179–202.

47. *DA*, pp. 31–80.

48. *Lucians Rezension der Königsbücher*, pp. 265–267.

49. *The Septuagint and Jewish Worship*, pp. 17–18; *DA*, p. 36.

50. For arguments in favor of attributing II Samuel 10: 1–11: 1 to the KR see Appendix B.

51. Citations from the MT are taken from the third edition of Kittel's *Biblia Hebraica*, 3rd. ed. (Stuttgart, 1937); citations from the Greek texts are taken from *The Old Testament in Greek*, ed. Alan E. Brooke, Norman McLean, H. St. J. Thackeray, vol. II: *The Later Historical Books*, pt. 1: *I and II Samuel* (London,

1927); pt. 2: *I and II Kings* (London, 1930). The numbering of the verses will follow that of the MT.

52. B text: II Sam. 11:27; 15:25; I Kings 22:43; II Kings 3:2, 18; 13:2, 11; 14:3; 15:3, 9, 18, 24, 28, 34; 16:2; 17:2, 17; 18:3; 21:2, 6, 16, 20; 22:2, 23:32, 37; 24:9.
    L text: II Kings 15:18; 16:2; 21:16.

53. B text: I Sam. 12:17; 15:19; 26:24; I Kings 3:10; 11:6; 14:22; 15:5, 11, 26, 34; 16:7, 19, 25, 30; 21:20, 25; II Kings 8:18, 27; 12:3; 14:24; 24:19.
    L text: I Sam. 12:17; 15:19; II Sam. 11:27; 15:25; I Kings 3:10; 11:6; 14:22; 15:5, 11, 26, 34; 16:7, 19, 25, 30; 21:20, 25; 22:53; II Kings 3:2, 18; 8:18, 27; 12:3; 13:2, 11; 14:3, 24; 15:3, 9, 24, 28, 34; 17:2, 17; 18:3; 21:2, 6, 20; 22:2; 23:32, 37; 24:9, 19.

54. B text: I Kings 22:53.
    L text: I Sam. 26:24.

55. B text: II Sam. 10:12; 12:9; 15:26; II Kings 10:30; 20:3; 21:15.
    L text: II Sam. 10:12; II Kings 10:30; 20:3; 21:15.

56. B text: I Sam. 3:18; II Sam. 7:19; I Kings 11:33, 38.
    L text: I Sam. 3:18; II Sam. 7:19; 12:9; 15:26; I Kings 11:33, 38.

57. B text: I Sam. 1:18, 23; 8:6; 16:22; 18:8, 20, 23, 26; 20:3, 29; 24:5; 25:8; 26:21, 24; 27:5; 29:6*bis*, 7, 9; II Sam. 3:19*bis*; 6:22; 11:25; 13:2; 14:22; 16:4; 17:4*bis*; 18:4; 19:7, 19, 28, 38, 39; 24:22; II Kings 1:13, 14; 10:5.
    L text: I Sam. 1:18; 16:22; 18:5, 20, 23, 26; 20:3, 29; 24:5; 25:8; 26:21, 24; 27:5; 29:6*bis*, 7, 9; II Sam. 3:19; 6:22; 13:2; 14:22; 16:4, 17:4*bis*; 19:19; II Kings 1:13, 14; 10:5.

58. B text: I Sam. 11:10; 14:36, 40; 15:17; 21:14; II Sam. 3:36*bis*; 4:10; 10:3; I Kings 21:2.
    L text: I Sam. 1:23; 8:6; 11:10; 14:36, 40; 15:17; 18:5, 8; 21:14; II Sam. 3:36*bis*; 4:10; 10:3; 11:25; 18:4; 19:7, 38, 39; 24:22; I Kings 21:2.

59. B text: I Kings 11:19.
    L text: I Kings 11:19.

60. A good example in the γδ′ section of Kings is the lack of consistency in carrying out the KR revision for the Hebrew word מַעַל: "Il est difficile de dire pourquoi certains ἀπό sont demeurés sans correction" (*DA*, p. 56).

61. B text: I Sam. 1:3, 4, 21; 2:13, 15, 19; 11:15; 15:15; 16:2, 5; 28:24. I Kings 3:3, 4; 8:5, 62, 63*bis*; 11:8; 12:32; 13:2; 19:21. II Kings 17:36.
    L text: I Sam. 1:3, 4, 21; 2:13, 15, 19; 6:15; 10:8; 11:15; 15:15, 21; 16:2, 5; 28:24. II Sam. 15:12. I Kings 1:9, 19, 25; 3:2, 3, 4; 8:5, 62, 63*bis*; 11:8; 12:32; 13:2; 19:21. II Kings 15:4, 35; 17:35, 36; 23:20.

62. B text: II Sam. 15:12. I Kings 1:9, 19, 25; II Kings 12:4; 14:4; 15:4, 35; 16:4; 17:35; 23:20.
    L text: II Kings 12:4; 14:4; 16:4 (but r has ἔθυεν).

63. See Cross, "History of the Biblical Text," p. 296; *Ancient Library*, pp. 190–192.

64. For a recent study of the asterisked additions to the Septuagint see Soisalon-Soininen, *Der Charakter der asterisierten Zusätze*, and the detailed and critical review of this book by D. W. Gooding in *Gnomon*, 30 (1961), 143–148. For an exemplary discussion of the hexaplaric text in I Samuel see Johnson, *Die Hexaplarische Rezension*.

65. This question has been studied for the Books of Kings by Wevers in "A Study in the Textual History of Codex Vaticanus in the Books of Kings," *ZAW*, 64 (1952), 178–189.

66. This is very frequently the case with the minuscule c_2. Johnson considers this manuscript to be the most important witness to the hexaplaric signs in I Samuel (*Die Hexaplarische Rezension*, p. 25).

67. *DA*, pp. 15–21.

68. *Ibid.*, pp. 81–88.

69. *Ibid.*, pp. 142–143.

70. "The So-called Quinta of 4 Kings," *Proceedings of the Society of Biblical Archaeology*, 24 (1902), 216–219.

71. See the remarks of S. P. Brock in his review of Johnson's *Die Hexaplarische Rezension*, (*Journal of Theological Studies*, 15, 1964, 115).

72. For the hexaplaric witnesses in I Samuel see Johnson, *Die Hexaplarische Rezension*; for I Kings see the older study of Siegfried Silberstein, "Über den Ursprung der im Codex Alexandrinus und Vaticanus des dritten Königsbuches der alexandrinischen Übersetzung überlieferten Textgestalt," *ZAW*, 13 (1893), 1–75; 14 (1894), 1–30. For the best hexaplaric witnesses in the sections of Samuel and Kings belonging to the KR see *DA*, pp. 138–139. Wevers lists the best hexaplaric witnesses for Kings as: A x Armenian Syrohexapla ("Proto-Septuagint Studies," p. 59, n. 6).

73. Cf. H. S. Gehman, "The Armenian Version of I and II Kings," *JAOS*, 54 (1934), 53–59.

74. For a recent revival of interest in this recension see Sidney Jellicoe, "The Hesychian Recension Reconsidered," *JBL*, 82 (1963), 409–418; and A. Vaccari, "The Hesychian Recension of the Septuagint," *Biblica*, 46 (1965), 60–66.

75. See, however, the discussion of the Lucianic manuscript c_2 in the following chapter.

Notes to Chapter II

1. These two types are conveniently classified and analyzed by Otto Eissfeldt in *The Old Testament: An Introduction*, trans. Peter R. Ackroyd (New York, 1965), pp. 282–297.

2. See James A. Montgomery, *A Critical and Exegetical Commentary on the Books of Kings*, International Critical Commentary (Edinburgh, 1951), pp. 39–41.

3. A concise treatment of the regnal formulae is given by C. F. Burney in *Notes on the Hebrew Text of the Books of Kings*, (Oxford, 1903), pp. ix–xii.

4. Samuel R. Driver, *An Introduction to the Literature of the Old Testament*, 9th ed., (Edinburgh, 1913), p. 189.

5. The MT has the concluding part of the regnal formula of Joash following immediately upon the introductory part (II Kings 13: 10–13), leaving outside the framework of the regnal formula (II Kings 13: 14–25) the supplementary material concerning Joash's reign. The arrangement of L is clearly superior. The supplementary material concerning Joash's reign is enclosed between the introductory regnal formula (II Kings 13: 10–11) and the concluding regnal formula (II Kings 13: 25+). A second version of the concluding part of Joash's regnal formula is also found in chapter 14. In the MT it comprises two verses (II Kings 14: 15–16), whereas L has only a single verse (II Kings 14: 16).

6. *The Mysterious Numbers*, 2nd ed., pp. 16–38.

7. At II Kings 15: 30 the MT has a supplementary synchronism that is incompatible with the remainder of the data in its chronological system. Hoshea is said to have assassinated and succeeded Pekah to the throne in the twentieth year of Jotham. L does not have this additional synchronism.

8. Cf. Vannutelli, *Libri synoptici*, p. vi.

9. For two recent attempts to untangle the complicated chronology of the period of Pekah see H. J. Cook, "Pekah," *VT*, 14 (1964), 121–135; Thiele, "Pekah to Hezekiah," *VT*, 16 (1966), 83–103.

10. Olmstead ("Source Study," pp. 15–30) provides a lengthy defense of the antiquity of this doublet. Montgomery (*Commentary*, pp. 251–254) gives a detailed review of the scholarly opinion on the significance of this doublet for the development of the Greek text.

11. The minuscules that omit the whole section 12: 24^{a-z} are: efmqstwxy; the verses 12: 24^{g-z} are omitted by dp.

12. F. C. Burkitt, in his publication of the Aquila fragments from the Cairo Genizah (*Fragments of the Books of Kings According to the Translation of Aquila*, Cambridge, Eng., 1897, pp. 33 f.), attempts to show that the hexaplaric text is not an extract from Aquila but is the Old Greek text from 12: 24^{g-n} amended into general accord with Aquila. Approximately the same conclusion is reached by Joseph Reider in his *Prolegomena to a Greek-Hebrew and Hebrew-Greek Index to Aquila*, (Philadelphia, 1916), pp. 156–158.

13. It was Thiele's failure to distinguish the recensional stages in the development of the Greek text that led him to find inconsistency in the Greek data for the reign of Jeroboam: "As the Greek data for this period are examined, however, it will be noticed that there are certain inconsistencies. For instance, the official length of Jeroboam's reign is given as twenty-two years, but the accession of Asa is synchronized with Jeroboam's twenty-fourth year." (*The Mysterious Numbers*, 1st ed., p. 171). Thiele has not seen that the data concerning the number of regnal years of Jeroboam have been taken from the hexaplaric recension (= MT),

whereas the synchronism is taken from the Old Greek and Lucianic texts, which do not have the number of regnal years for Jeroboam.

14. Thiele, *The Mysterious Numbers*, 1st ed., p. 171.

15. *Ibid.*, p. 169.

16. *Ibid.*, pp. 171–172.

17. See Thiele's chart, *ibid.*, p. 171.

18. See Thiele's explanation of the MT data (*ibid.*, p. 190).

19. For the authenticity of the notice, see Burney, *Notes* p. 203.

20. Several Greek manuscripts (N*vxy) have actually corrected the accession year of Omri at I Kings 16: 23 to the twenty-seventh year of Asa in an effort to make sense of the data of the MT.

21. See the discussion by Bernhard Stade and the evidence he adduces for the antiquity of the order of the Old Greek text in *The Books of Kings*, The Sacred Books of the Old Testament (Leipzig, 1904), pp. 148, 176.

22. Montgomery (*Commentary*, p. 347) is skeptical about the regnal formula of Jehoshaphat at 16: 28^(a–h), suggesting that it may be entirely artificial.

Notes to Chapter III

1. Even Thiele has realized that the conflicting data in the doublet regnal formula for Jehoshaphat must stem from two incompatible chronologies, one early and the other late. His bias in favor of the data of the MT, however, and his indifference to the historical development of the Greek text incline him to regard the data in the Greek text that agrees with the MT as early, whereas the data of the Old Greek and proto-Lucian texts are considered to be late (*The Mysterious Numbers*, 1st ed., p. 191), a conclusion that is diametrically opposed to the actual case as the present investigation will show.

2. Synchronism first: II Kings 12: 2; 13: 1, 10; 14: 1, 23; 15: 1, 8, 17, 23, 27, 32; 16: 1; 17: 1; 18: 1.

Name of king first: II Kings 15: 13.

3. Synchronism first: I Kings 15: 1, 9, 33; 16: 8, 15, 23.

Name of king first: 15: 25.

4. Thackeray, *The Septuagint and Jewish Worship*, pp. 20–22, 115. Barthélemy, *DA*, pp. 63–65.

5. I Kings 15: 1, 8, 9, 24, 25, 33; 16: 6, 23*bis*, 28, 29. The two occurrences of מלך in the regnal formula of Rehoboam (14: 21), as well as the verb form וימלך (14: 31), are translated by the aorist in both the Old Greek and Lucianic texts.

6. I Kings 15: 1, 9, 25, 33; 16: 23, 29.

7. I Kings 16: 23. This second instance of the verb βασιλεύει in this verse is found in a supplementary notice concerning the reign of Omri at Tirzah before the transfer of his capital to Samaria.

8. I Kings 15: 8, 24; 16: 6, 28. The aorist is used, however, for this verb at 14: 31 in the concluding regnal formula of Rehoboam.

9. I Kings 1: 11, 13, 18; II Kings 9: 13.

10. *DA*, pp. 64–65.

11. For a similar view see Stade, *The Books of Kings*, pp. 148, 176.

12. Cf. Soisalon-Soininen, *Der Charakter der asterisierten Zusätze in der Septuaginta*, p. 70.

13. Dative: 15: 2; 18: 2; 21: 1, 19; 22: 1; 23: 31, 36; 24: 8, 18. Genitive 8: 26; 12: 2(1); 14: 2; 15: 33.

14. See Stade, *The Books of Kings*, p. 176, for typical usage in regnal formulae.

15. The significance of the expression in question for distinguishing differences in recension has been noticed by several scholars with precise reference to the present texts (I Kings 16: 28[b] = I Kings 22: 43). See Stade, *ibid.*; Rahlfs, *Lucians Rezension der Königsbücher*, p. 266; Olmstead, "The Earliest Book of Kings," p. 178.

16. I Kings 15: 14; II Kings 12: 4; 14: 4; 15: 4; 15: 35.

17. For a full discussion of the translation practice of the Greek texts over against the MT see Stade, *The Books of Kings*, p. 141.

18. II Kings 12: 4; 14: 4; 15: 4, 35.

19. The expression, καὶ ὅσα ἐπολέμησεν, is under the asterisk in A, the Armenian, and the Syrohexapla at 22: 46.

20. Cf. Georg Beer, *Hebräische Grammatik*, 2nd rev. ed. by Rudolf Meyer (Berlin, 1952), pp. 119–120.

21. Cf. Swete, *Introduction*, p. 41.

22. Cf. Soisalon-Soininen, *Der Charakter der asterisierten Zusätze*, p. 145; Joseph Reider and Nigel Turner, *An Index to Aquila*, Supplements to *VT*, 12. Leiden, 1966, p. 51.

23. *DA*, pp. 59–60.

24. *The Books of Kings*, p. 177.

Notes to Chapter IV

1. Thackeray, *The Septuagint and Jewish Worship*, pp. 19–20; *DA*, p. 142.

2. *DA*, pp. 48–54.

3. This same conclusion had already been reached by Stade, *The Books of Kings*, p. 176.

4. See also Stade, *ibid.*, pp. 177–178.

5. The two words in question are found under the obelus in the Syrohexapla.

6. See Burney, *Notes*, p. 261.

7. *Lucians Rezension der Königsbücher*, p. 287.

8. *Ibid.*, pp. 287–288.

9. The readings of the various manuscripts are:
    B ἐναντίον
    N ἔναντι
    boc₂e₂ A eimouv ἐνώπιον
10. Cf. the table in Chapter II where the comparative data of the Greek and Hebrew chronologies are given.
11. See Stade, *The Books of Kings*, p. 181; Olmstead, "The Earliest Book of Kings," pp. 178–179.
12. *Lucians Rezension der Königsbücher*, pp. 266–267.
13. *Ibid.*, p. 271.
14. *Ibid.*, p. 267.
15. Barthélemy suggests that the same practice was followed in the KR revision of II Samuel (*DA*, p. 65).
16. This hypothesis is defended by Thiele in *The Mysterious Numbers of the Hebrew Kings*, 1st ed., pp. 191–200; and in a later article, "The Question of Coregencies among the Hebrew Kings," *A Stubborn Faith*. Papers on Old Testament and Related Subjects Presented to Honor William Andrew Irwin, ed. E. C. Hobbs (Dallas, 1956), pp. 41–43.
17. Thiele, *The Mysterious Numbers*, 1st ed., p. 13.
18. *Ibid.*, pp. 196–197.
19. Thiele, "The Question of Coregencies," pp. 41–43.
20. Thiele himself is the first to admit the inferential character of his argument for a coregency for Jehoram: "By following certain hints and suggestions, by noticing a faint inference here and a slight indication there, the mind is first drawn out toward various hypotheses and later to more solid conclusions, until at length solutions are reached to some of our most difficult problems. Let us take, for instance, the matter of coregencies. Must we deny the existence of any coregency unless ancient records explicitly tell us that it took place?" *ibid.*, pp. 39–40.
21. According to Thiele (*ibid.*, pp. 41–43) the accession of Joram of Israel would have been synchronized first with Jehoram of Judah, as coregent with Jehoshaphat (MT II Kings 1:17b=II Kings 1:18ᵃ in L), and in the doublet regnal formula (MT and B at II Kings 3:1–3) with Jehoshaphat also, without any reference to Jehoram. No explanation is given for such an unprecedented double synchronism, even if the existence of a coregency were to be granted.
22. Cf. also the historical present θάπτουσιν in the concluding verse of this passage peculiar to L.
23. This diagram is a synthesis of chronological data found only in L (boe₂).
24. "The Question of Coregencies," p. 41.
25. *Ibid.*, p. 42.
26. Both Stade (*The Books of Kings*, p. 217) and Burney (*Notes*, p. 294) observe that the clause in question is a late corruption occasioned by the similarity of the clause at the end of the same verse. The clause is found in B A boc₂e₂ and the Ethiopian; it is omitted by N rell Armenian, Old Latin and the Syrohexapla.
27. *The Mysterious Numbers*, 2nd ed., pp. 181–182.

Notes to Chapter V

1. See Eissfeldt, *The Old Testament*, pp. 282–297; Burney, *Notes*, pp. 207–215; Gray, *I and II Kings*, pp. 335–337 and 415–421.

2. See Burney, *Notes*, p. 210. For the opposite view see D. W. Gooding, "Ahab According to the Septuagint," *ZAW*, 76 (1964), 269–279).

3. *The Old Testament*, p. 294.

4. Eissfeldt suggests that the narratives in II Kings 5, 6: 8–23, and 6: 24–7: 19, which depict Elisha in a friendly relation with the king of Israel, cannot refer to a son of Ahab but must originally have referred to Jehu, Jehoahaz, or Joash (*ibid.*, p. 296). An even more radical revision of the identifications of the kings of Israel in the Elijah–Elisha narratives is proposed by C. F. Whitley in "The Deuteronomic Presentation of the House of Omri," *VT*, 2 (1952), 137–152. See now also J. Maxwell Miller, "The Elisha Cycle and the Accounts of the Omride Wars," *JBL*, 85 (1966), 441–454.

5. See H. Donner and W. Röllig, *Kanaanäische und Aramäische Inschriften*, II, *Kommentar* (Wiesbaden, 1964), 168–179. The most recent comprehensive study of the Moabites, with an extensive bibliography, is the monograph of A. H. Van Zyl, *The Moabites* (Leiden, 1960). For linguistic aspects of the Mesha inscription see Stanislav Segert, "Die Sprache der moabitischen Königsinschrift," *Archiv Orientalni*, 29, (1961), 197–267. The most recent treatment of line eight in the Mesha inscription is by Gerhard Wallis, "Die vierzig Jahre der achten Zeile der Mesa-Inschrift," *Zeitschrift des Deutschen Palästina-Vereins*, 81 (1965), 180–186. The historical background of the inscription is discussed by J. Liver, "The Wars of Mesha, King of Moab," *Palestine Exploration Quarterly*, 99 (1967), 14–31.

6. For the translation "his son" see Frank M. Cross, Jr., and David Noel Freedman, *Early Hebrew Orthography*, American Oriental Series, 36 (New Haven, 1952), p. 39.

7. "The Mesha Stone nowhere names this king [against whom Mesha revolted], but indicates that he is the 'son of Omri' and 'succeeded him' to the throne of Israel. This in itself is not decisive, however, since the word *ben* has a variety of meanings, and in the Bible is used to designate grandchildren and descendants generally, as well as sons" (*ibid.*).

8. "That the king in question is actually the last of the house of Omri is implied in line 7, where we have an allusion to the overthrow of the Omride dynasty (cf. Montgomery, *The Books of Kings*, ICC, 1951, pp. 358–359). In the inscription then, Mesha has passed over from Omri, who conquered the land, to Joram, in whose day the Moabites regained their independence" (*ibid.*).

9. The anonymous king of Israel is mentioned in the following places: II Kings 5: 5, 6, 7, 8; 6: 9, 10, 11, 12, 21, 26, 28, 30; 7: 6, 12, 14, 15, 17, 18; 8: 3, 4, 5, 6; 13: 16, 18.

10. Contrast the account of the revolt of Jehu, in which Elisha the prophet is a secondary figure. The kings of Israel and Judah are here specifically mentioned: II Kings 9: 14, 15, 16, 17, 21, 22, 23, 24, 27.

11. The kings of Israel and Judah are identified in either the MT or in L in seven verses in chapter 3 (II Kings 3: 6, 7, 8, 9, 11, 12, 14) and only once elsewhere (II Kings 13: 14).

12. In reviewing the data for the distribution of the identifications of the kings of Israel and Judah in this and the following notes, the first number indicates the verse, and the second number the subdivision of the verse according to the presentation of the comparative texts in the preceding pages: 6, 3; 9, 2; 10, 2; 11, 10; 12, 6; 13, 2; 13, 10.

13. 9, 2; 10, 2; 11, 10; 12, 6; 13, 2; 13, 10.

14. 7, 4; 9, 4; 11, 2; 12, 2; 12, 8; 14, 9.

15. Cf. Begrich, *Die Chronologie*, pp. 166–167.

16. See, for example, the discussion of Elijah's letter in the commentary of Wilhelm Rudolph, *Chronikbücher*, Handbuch zum alten Testament (Tübingen, 1955), p. 267; and in the notes to the translation of Jacob M. Myers, *II Chronicles*, The Anchor Bible (New York, 1965), pp. 121–122.

17. Rudolph has at least recognized the possibility that the Chronicler was following a chronology, based on the data in the MT at II Kings 1: 17b, which would have allowed Elijah to have witnessed the crimes of Jehoram (*Chronikbücher*, p. 267).

18. Even if the story about Elijah's letter to Jehoram were a complete fabrication on the part of the Chronicler, he would have been all the more careful that his story possessed the verisimilitude of conforming to the accepted chronology of his time, according to which Elijah and Jehoram were contemporaries. It is arbitrary, however, to consider any narrative of the Chronicler to be legendary because it has no parallel in Samuel and Kings. For a recent study which reevaluates the historical worth of Chronicles on the basis of manuscript discoveries from Qumran see Werner E. Lemke, "The Synoptic Problem in the Chronicler's History," *HTR*, 38 (1965), 349–363.

19. No altogether satisfactory explanation of the reference to the king of Edom in II Kings 3: 26 has as yet been given. Montgomery (*Commentary*, p. 363), following the lead of Winckler and a reading in the Old Latin (*Syriae*), has suggested that the original reference was to the king of Aram, which reading was later easily corrupted into Edom. However this may be, the first two references (verses 9 and 12) are to the king of Edom.

20. The Greek texts are of little assistance here. The Old Greek at I Kings 16: 28ᵉ has simply transliterated the word it did not understand: ναϲειβ ὁ βαϲιλεύϲ. In the doublet at I Kings 22: 48 the word which was transliterated in the Old Greek has been given the characteristic rendition of Aquila: ἐϲτηλωμένοϲ.

21. "Miscellen," *ZAW*, 4 (1884), 178.

22. John Gray, *I and II Kings*, The Old Testament Library (Philadelphia, 1964), p. 434.

23. *Ibid.*, p. 481.
24. For this aspect of the Deuteronomist's theology of history see Gerhard von Rad, *Studies in Deuteronomy* (London, 1953), pp. 84–86.
25. Begrich, who also holds for the late insertion of the proper names in II Kings 3, has stressed the acceptability of Jehoshaphat from the religious viewpoint (*Die Chronologie*, p. 167).
26. This is also the view of Rahlfs. His other suggestion is that the Lucianic redactor may have simply wished to avoid having the kings of both Israel and Judah with the same name, which would have been the case had the king of Judah been identified with Jehoram. In either case, Rahlfs, in line with his bias against the antiquity of the Lucianic tradition, believes that the name of Ahaziah in L is a late alteration of the MT (*Lucians Rezension der Königsbücher*, pp. 271–272).

Notes to Appendix A

1. B Text: I Sam. 7: 11; 17: 52; 23: 25, 28; 24: 15; 25: 29; 26: 18, 20; 30: 8*bis*. II Sam. 2: 19, 24, 28; 17: 1; 20: 6. I Kings 20: 20.
   L Text: I Sam. 7: 11; 17: 15; 23: 25, 28; 24: 15; 25: 29; 26: 18, 20; 30: 8*bis*, 10. II Sam. 2: 19, 24, 28; 18: 16; 20: 6, 7, 10, 13; 24: 13. I Kings 20: 20. II Kings 5: 21; 9: 27; 25: 5.
2. B Text: I Sam. 30: 10. II Sam. 18: 16; 20: 7, 10, 13; 22: 38; 24: 13. II Kings 5: 21; 9: 27; 25: 5.
   L Text: None.
3. B Text: I Sam. 12: 9; 14: 50; 26: 5. II Sam. 2: 8. I Kings 2: 32*bis*.
   L Text: I Sam. 12: 9; 14: 50; 26: 5. II Sam. 2: 8; 10: 16, 18; 19: 14. I Kings 1: 19, 25; 2: 5, 32*bis*; II Kings 5: 1; 25: 19.
4. B Text: II Sam. 10: 16, 18; 19: 14. I Kings 1: 19, 25; 2: 5. II Kings 4: 13; 5: 1; 25: 19.
   L Text: II Kings 4: 13.
5. B Text: I Kings 3: 12, 28; 5: 9, 10*bis*, 21; 10: 4, 6, 8, 23, 24; 11: 41.
   L Text: II Sam. 13: 3; 14: 2, 20*bis*; 20: 22. I Kings 2: 6; 3: 12, 28; 5: 9, 10*bis*, 21; 10: 4, 6, 8, 23, 24; 11: 41.
6. B text: II Sam. 13: 3; 14: 2, 20*bis*; 20: 16, 22. I Kings 2: 6, 9; 5: 11, 14*bis*, 26.
   L text: II Sam. 20: 16. I Kings 2: 9; 5: 10, 11, 14*bis*, 26.
7. B Text: II Sam. 13: 20; 19: 11. II Kings 18: 36.
   L Text: I Sam. 10: 27.
8. B Text: none.
   L Text: II Sam. 13: 20; 19: 11. II Kings 18: 36.
9. B Text: I Kings 22: 3. II Kings 2: 3, 5; 7: 9.
   L Text: I Kings 22: 3. II Kings 2: 3, 5; 7: 9.

10. B Text: I Sam. 3: 13, 14; 20: 8; 25: 24; 28: 10. II Sam. 3: 8; 14: 32.
    I Kings 17: 18.
    L Text: I Sam. 3: 13; 20: 8; 25: 24; 28: 10. II Sam. 3: 8; 14: 9, 32; 19: 20;
    24: 10; I Kings 17: 18; II Kings 7: 9.
11. B Text: II Sam. 14: 9; 19: 20; 22: 24; 24: 10. II Kings 7: 9.
    L Text: II Sam. 22: 24.
12. B Text: I Sam. 4: 14; 23: 27; 25: 18, 23, 34; 28: 20, 24. I Kings 20: 41.
    II Kings 9: 13.
    L Text: I Sam. 4: 14; 23: 27; 25: 18, 23, 34; 28: 20, 24. II Sam. 15: 14;
    19: 17. I Kings 20: 33, 41. II Kings 9: 13.
13. B Text: II Sam. 15: 14*bis*; 19: 17. I Kings 22: 9.
    L Text: I Sam. 9: 12; 17: 48; 25: 42. I Kings 22: 9.
14. B Text: I Sam. 1: 20; 4: 19.
    L Text: I Sam. 1: 20; 2: 21; 4: 19. II Sam. 11: 5*bis*; II Kings 4: 17.
15. B Text: II Sam. 11: 5*bis*. II Kings 4: 17; 8: 12; 15: 16.
    L Text: II Kings 8: 12; 15: 16.
16. B Text: I Sam. 15: 9; 22: 17; 31: 4. II Sam. 6: 10.
    L Text: I Sam. 15: 9; 22: 17; 31: 4. II Sam. 6: 10, 12: 17; 13: 14, 16, 25;
    23: 16, 17.
17. B Text: I Sam. 26: 23. II Sam. 2: 21; 12: 17; 13: 14, 16, 25; 14: 29*bis*;
    23: 16, 17. I Kings 20: 8. II Kings 8: 19; 13: 23; 24: 4.
    L Text: I Sam. 26: 23. II Sam. 2: 21; 14: 29*bis*; I Kings 20: 8. II Kings
    8: 19; 13: 23; 24: 4.

Bibliography

Albright, William F. "The Chronology of the Divided Monarchy of Israel," *BASOR*, 100 (1945), 16–22.

———— "Alternative Chronology," *Interpretation*, 6 (1952), 101–103.

———— "New Light on Early Recensions of the Hebrew Bible," *BASOR*, 140 (1955), 27–33.

———— "The Original Account of the Fall of Samaria in II Kings," *BASOR*, 174 (1964), 66–67.

Baars, W. "A Forgotten Fragment of the Greek Text of the Books of Samuel," *Oudtestamentische Studiën*, 14 (1965), 201–205.

Baillet, Maurice, et al. "Editing the Manuscript Fragments from Qumran," *Biblical Archaeologist*, 19 (1956), 75–96.

————, J. T. Milik, and R. de Vaux, *Discoveries in the Judean Desert of Jordan*, III: *Les "Petites Grottes" de Qumran*. Oxford, 1962.

Bardy, Gustave. *Recherches sur Saint Lucien d'Antioche et son école*. Paris, 1936.

Barnes, W. E. "The Peshitta Version of 2K," *Journal of Theological Studies*, 6 (1905), 220–232; 11 (1910), 533–542.

Barthélemy, Dominique. "Redécouverte d'un chaînon manquant de l'histoire de la septante," *RB*, 60 (1953), 18–29.

———— "Quinta ou Version selon les Hébreux," *Theologische Zeitschrift* (Basel), 16 (1960), 342–353.

———— *Les Devanciers d'Aquila*. Supplements to *VT*, 10. Leiden, 1963.

Begrich, Joachim. *Die Chronologie der Könige von Israel und Juda*. Beiträge zur historischen Theologie, No. 3. Tübingen, 1929.

Bertram, Georg. "Zur Septuaginta-Forschung. I. Textausgaben der Septuaginta," *Theologische Rundschau*, N.F. 3 (1931), 283–296.

———— "Zur Septuaginta-Forschung. II. Das Textproblem der Septuaginta," *Theologische Rundschau*, N. F. 5 (1933), 173–186.

———— "Zur Septuaginta-Forschung. III. Das Problem der Umschrifttexte," *Theologische Rundschau*, N. F. 10 (1938), 69–80, 133–159.

Bič, Miloš. "Die Glaubwürdigkeit des massoretischen Textes und des der Septuaginta im Licht der Qumranfunde," *Communio Viatorum*, 3 (1960), 158–172.

Bickerman, Elias. "The Septuagint as a Translation," *Proceedings of the American Academy of Jewish Research*, 28 (1959), 1–39.

de Boer, P. A. H. *Research into the Text of 1 Samuel I–XVI*. Amsterdam, 1938.

———— "I Samuel 17. Notes on the Text and the Ancient Versions," *Oudtestamentische Studiën*, 1 (1942), 79–104.

———— "Research into the Text of I Samuel XVII–XXXI," *Oudtestamentische Studiën*, 6 (1949), 1–100.

Brock, S. P. Review of Bo Johnson, *Die Hexaplarische Rezension des 1 Samuelbuches der Septuaginta* in *Journal of Theological Studies*, 15 (1964), 112–117.

Brownlee, W. H. *The Meaning of the Qumran Scrolls for the Bible*. New York, 1964.

Burkitt, F. C. *Fragments of the Books of Kings according to the Translation of Aquila*. Cambridge, 1897.

———— "The So-called Quinta of 4 Kings," *Proceedings of the Society of Biblical Archaeology*, 24 (1902), 216–219.

———— "The Lucianic Text of I Kings 8: 53b," *Journal of Theological Studies*, 10 (1909), 439–446.

Burney, C. F. *Notes on the Hebrew Text of the Books of Kings*. Oxford, 1903.

Campbell, Edward F., and David N. Freedman. "The Chronology of Israel and the Ancient Near East," *The Bible and the Ancient Near East*, ed. G. E. Wright. New York, 1961, pp. 203–228.

Chapman, W. J. "Zum Ursprung der chronologischen Angabe I Kings 6, 1," *ZAW*, 53 (1935), 185–189.

Cook, H. J. "Pekah," *VT*, 14 (1964), 121–135.

Cook, S. A. "Notes on the Dynasties of Omri and Jehu," *Jewish Quarterly Review*, 20 (1908), 597–630.

Cooper, C. M. "Theodotion's Influence on the Alexandrian Text of Judges," *JBL*, 67 (1948), 63–68.

Coppens, J. "La Critique textuelle de l'ancien testament: solutions anciennes et données nouvelles," *Ephemerides Theologicae Lovanienses*, 36 (1960), 466–475.

Coste, J. "La Première Expérience de traduction biblique: la septante," *La Maison-Dieu*, 53 (1958), 56–88.

Cross, Frank M., Jr. "A New Qumran Biblical Fragment Related to the Original Hebrew Underlying the Septuagint," *BASOR*, 132 (1953), 15–26.

———— "The Oldest Manuscripts from Qumran," *JBL*, 74 (1955), 142–172.

———— *The Ancient Library of Qumran and Modern Biblical Studies*, 2nd ed. New York, 1961.

———— "The History of the Biblical Text in the Light of Discoveries in the Judean Desert," *HTR*, 57 (1964), 281–299.

———— "The Contribution of the Qumran Discoveries to the Study of the Biblical Text," *Israel Exploration Journal*, 16 (1966), 81–95.

———— and David N. Freedman. *Early Hebrew Orthography*. New Haven, 1952.

Daniel, Suzanne. *Recherches sur le vocabulaire du culte dans la Septante.* Etudes et Commentaires LXI. Paris, 1966.

Dieu, L. "Les Manuscrits grecs des Livres de Samuel," *Le Muséon*, 34 (1921), 17–60.

Donner, H. and W. Röllig. *Kanaanäische und Aramäische Inschriften.* 3 vols. Wiesbaden, 1964.

Dörrie, Heinrich. "Zur Geschichte der Septuaginta im Jahrhundert Konstantins," *ZNW*, 39 (1940), 57–110.

Driver, S. R. *An Introduction to the Literature of the Old Testament*, 9th ed. Edinburgh, 1913.

―――― *Notes on the Hebrew Text and the Topography of the Books of Samuel*, 2nd ed. Oxford, 1913.

Eissfeldt, Otto. *The Old Testament: An Introduction*, trans. from the third German edition by Peter R. Ackroyd. New York, 1965.

Eybers, I. H. "Notes on the Texts of Samuel found in Qumran Cave 4," *Studies on the Books of Samuel*, Pretoria, 1960, pp. 1–17.

Fischer, Bonafatius. "Lukian-Lesarten in der Vetus Latina der vier Königsbücher," *Miscellanea Biblica et Orientalia R. P. Athanasio Miller O. S. B. Oblata*. Rome, 1951, pp. 169–177.

Gehman, H. S. "The Old Ethiopic Version of I Kings and its Affinities," *JBL*, 50 (1931), 81–114.

―――― "The Armenian Version of I and II Kings and its Affinities," *JAOS*, 54 (1934), 53–59.

―――― "Exegetical Methods Employed by the Greek Translator of 1 Samuel," *JAOS*, 70 (1950) 292–296.

Gerleman, Gillis. *Studies in the Septuagint. II. Chronicles.* Lunds Universitets Arsskrift, N. F., avd. 1, bd. 43, nr. 3. Lund, 1946.

―――― *Synoptic Studies in the Old Testament.* Lunds Universitets Arsskrift, N. F., avd. 1, bd. 44, nr. 5. Lund, 1948.

Gooding, D. W. *Recensions of the Septuagint Pentateuch.* London, 1955.

―――― *The Account of the Tabernacle: Translation and Textual Problems of the Greek Exodus.* Cambridge, Eng., 1959.

―――― Review of Ilmari Soisalon-Soininen, *Der Charakter der asterisierten Zusätze in der Septuaginta* in *Gnomon*, 30 (1961), 143–148.

―――― "Aristeas and Septuagint Origins," *VT*, 13 (1963), 357–379.

―――― "Ahab According to the Septuagint," *ZAW*, 76 (1964), 269–279.

―――― "Temple Specifications: a Dispute in Logical Arrangement between the MT and the LXX," *VT*, 17 (1967), 143–172.

―――― "The Septuagint's Rival Versions of Jeroboam's Rise to Power," *VT*, 17 (1967), 173–189.

Goshen-Gottstein, Moshe. "Neue Syrohexaplarfragmente," *Biblica*, 37 (1956), 162–183.

―――― *Text and Language in Bible and Qumran.* Jerusalem, 1960.

———— "Theory and Practice of Textual Criticism." The Text-critical Use of the Septuagint," *Textus*, 3 (1963), 130–158.

————, ed. *The Book of Isaiah: Sample Edition with Introduction.* The Hebrew University Bible Project, Jerusalem, 1965.

———— "Hebrew Biblical Manuscripts. Their History and Their Place in the HUBP Edition," *Biblica*, 48 (1967), 243–290.

Gray, John. *I and II Kings: A Commentary.* Old Testament Library. London, 1964.

Greenberg, Moshe. "The Stabilization of the Text of the Hebrew Bible, Reviewed in the Light of the Biblical Materials from the Judean Desert," *JAOS*, 76 (1956), 157–167.

Grelot, Pierre. "Sur l'inspiration et la canonicité de la Septante," *Sciences Ecclésiastiques*, 16 (1964), 387–418.

———— "Les versions grecques de Daniel," *Biblica*, 47 (1966), 381–402.

Hänel, Johannes. "Die Zusätze der LXX in I Kings 2, 35^{a-o} und 46^{a-l}," *ZAW*, 47 (1929), 76–79.

Haupert, R. S. *The Relation of Codex Vaticanus and the Lucianic Text in the Books of the Kings from the Viewpoint of the Old Latin and the Ethiopic Versions.* Philadelphia, 1930.

Hautsch, Ernst. *Der Lukiantext des Oktateuch.* Mitteilungen der Septuaginta Unternehmens der königlichen Gesellschaft der Wissenschaften zu Göttingen, I, Berlin, 1910, 1–28.

Hedley, P. L. "The Göttingen Investigation and Edition of the Septuagint," *HTR*, 26 (1933), 57–72.

Hempel, Johannes. "Zum griechischen Deuteronomium Text des II Jahrhunderts a. C.," *ZAW*, 55 (1937), 115–127.

———— "Ein textgeschichtlich bedeutsamer Fund," *ZAW*, 65 (1954), 296–298.

Hrozny, Heinrich. *Die Abweichungen des Codex Vaticanus vom Hebräischen Texte in den Königsbüchern.* Leipzig, 1909.

Jellicoe, Sidney. "Aristeas, Philo and the Septuagint Vorlage," *Journal of Theological Studies*, 62 (1961), 261–271.

———— "The Hesychian Recension Reconsidered," *JBL*, 82 (1963), 409–418.

———— Review of Dominique Barthélemy, *Les Devanciers d'Aquila* in *JAOS*, 84 (1964), 178–182.

———— "The Septuagint To-day," *The Expository Times*, 77 (1965), 68–74.

———— "The Occasion and Purpose of the Letter of Aristeas: A Re-examination," *New Testament Studies*, 13 (1965–66), 144–150.

Jenni, Ernst. "Zwei Jahrzehnte Forschung an den Büchern Josua bis Könige," *Theologische Rundschau*, 27 (1961), 1–34, 97–146.

Jepsen, Alfred. *Die Quellen des Königsbuches*, 2nd ed. Halle-Salle, 1956.

———— "Von den Aufgaben der alttestamentlichen Textkritik," *Congress Volume Bonn 1962.* Supplements to *VT*, 9. Leiden, 1963, pp. 332–341.

———— and Robert Hanhart. *Untersuchungen zur israelitisch-jüdischen*

Chronologie. Beihefte zur *Zeitschrift für die alttestamentliche Wissenschaft,* 88. Berlin, 1964.

Johnson, Bo. *Die Hexaplarische Rezension des 1 Samuelbuches der LXX.* Studia Theologica Lundensia, 22. Lund, 1963.

Kahle, Paul. "Untersuchungen zur Geschichte des Pentateuchtextes," *Theologische Studien und Kritiken,* 88 (1915), 399–439.

——— "Die Septuaginta: Principielle Erwägungen," *Festschrift Otto Eissfeldt,* ed. J. Fück. Halle, 1947, pp. 161–180.

——— "Die im August 1952 entdeckte Lederrolle mit dem griechichen Text der kleinen Propheten und das Problem der Septuaginta," *Theologische Literaturzeitung,* 79 (1954), cols. 82–94.

——— "Problems of the Septuagint," *Studia Patristica,* I. Texte und Untersuchungen, 63. Berlin, 1957, pp. 328–338.

——— *The Cairo Genizah,* 2nd ed. Oxford, 1959.

——— "The Greek Bible Manuscripts Used by Origen," *JBL,* 79 (1960), 111–118.

Katz, Peter. "Das Problem des Urtextes der Septuaginta," *Theologische Zeitschrift,* 5 (1949), 1–24.

——— *Philo's Bible: The Aberrant Text of Bible Quotations in Some Philonic Writings and Its Place in the Textual History of the Greek Bible.* Cambridge, Eng., 1950.

——— "The Recovery of the Original Septuagint: A Study in the History of Transmission and Textual Criticism," *Actes du Ier Congrès de la Fédération Internationale des Associations d'Etudes Classiques.* Paris, 1951. pp. 165–182.

——— "Septuagintal Studies in the Mid-Century," *The Background of the New Testament and Its Eschatology,* ed. W. D. Davies and D. Daube. Cambridge, Eng., 1956, pp. 176–208.

——— "Justin's Old Testament Quotations and the Greek Dodekapropheton Scroll," *Studia Patristica,* I. Texte und Untersuchungen, 63. Berlin, 1957, pp. 243–253.

——— "Frühe hebraisierende Rezensionen der Septuaginta und die Hexapla," *ZAW,* 69 (1957), 77–84.

Katzenstein, H. J. "Who Were the Parents of Athaliah?" *Israel Exploration Journal,* 5 (1955), 194–197.

Kenyon, Frederick. *Our Bible and the Ancient Manuscripts,* 5th ed., revised and enlarged by A. W. Adams. London, 1958.

Klein, Ralph W. "New Evidence for an Old Recension of Reigns," *HTR,* 60 (1967), 93–105.

Klijn, A. F. J. "The Letter of Aristeas and the Greek Translation of the Pentateuch in Egypt," *New Testament Studies,* 11 (1964–65), 154–158.

Kraft, Robert A. Review of Dominique Barthélemy, *Les Devanciers d'Aquila* in *Gnomon,* 37 (1965), 474–483.

Kugler, F. X. *Von Moses bis Paulus.* Münster, 1922.

de Lagarde, Paul. *Anmerkungen zur griechischen Übersetzung der Proverbien.* Leipzig, 1963.

―――― *Ankündigung einer neuen Ausgabe der griechischen Übersetzung des alten Testaments.* Göttingen, 1882.

Lemke, Werner E. "The Synoptic Problem in the Chronicler's History," *HTR*, 38 (1965), 349–363.

Lewy, Julius. *Die Chronologie der Könige von Israel und Juda.* Giessen, 1927.

Lifschitz, B. "The Greek Documents from the Cave of Horror," *Israel Exploration Journal*, 12 (1962), 201–207.

Liver, J. "The Wars of Mesha, King of Moab," *Palestine Exploration Quarterly*, 99 (1967), 14–31.

Maass, Fritz. "Zu den Qumran-Varianten der Bücher Samuel," *Theologische Literaturzeitung*, 81 (1956), cols. 337–340.

Mansoor, Menahem. "The Massoretic Text in the Light of Qumran," *Congress Volume Bonn 1962.* Supplements to *VT*, 9. Leiden, 1963, pp. 305–321.

Margolis, Max L. *The Book of Joshua in Greek*, pts. I–IV. Paris, 1931–38.

Mercati, Giovanni. "Di alcune testimonianze antiche sulle cure bibliche di San Luciano," *Biblica*, 24 (1943), 1–17.

Metzger, Bruce. "Lucian and the Lucianic Recension," *New Testament Studies*, 8 (1961–62), 189–203.

―――― *Chapters in the History of New Testament Textual Criticism.* Leiden, 1963.

Mez, Adam. *Die Bibel des Josephus untersucht für Buch V–VII der Archäologie.* Basel, 1895.

Miller, J. Maxwell. "The Elisha Cycle and the Accounts of the Omride Wars," *JBL*, 85 (1966), 441–454.

―――― "The Fall of the House of Ahab," *VT*, 17 (1967) 307–324.

―――― "Another Look at the Chronology of the Early Divided Monarchy," *JBL*, 86 (1967), 276–288.

Montgomery, James. "The Supplement at the End of 3 Kingdoms 2," *ZAW*, 50 (1932), 124–129.

―――― "Archival Data in the Book of Kings," *JBL*, 53 (1934), 46–52.

―――― *A Critical and Exegetical Commentary of the Books of Kings.* International Critical Commentary. Edinburgh, 1951.

Moore, George. "The Antiochian Recension of the Septuagint," *American Journal of Semitic Languages and Literatures*, 29 (1912), 37–62.

Morenz, S. "Ägyptische Spuren in den Septuaginta," *Mullus. Festschrift Theodor Klauser. Jahrbuch für Antike und Christentum.* Ergänzungsband 1. Münster, 1964, pp. 250–258.

Morgenstern, Julian. "Chronological Data of the Dynasty of Omri," *JBL*, 59 (1940), 385–396.

Mowinckel, Sigmund. "Die Chronologie der israelitischen und jüdischen Könige," *Acta Orientalia (Leiden)*, 10 (1932), 161–277.

Myers, Jacob M. *II Chronicles: Translation and Notes.* The Anchor Bible. New York, 1965.

Napier, B. D. "The Omrides of Jezreel," *VT*, 9 (1959), 366–378.

Nyberg, H. S. "Das textkritische Problem des AT am Hoseabuche demonstriert," *ZAW*, 52 (1934), 241–254.

Olmstead, A. T. "Source Study and the Biblical Text," *American Journal of Semitic Languages and Literatures*, 30 (1913), 1–35.

―――― "The Earliest Book of Kings," *American Journal of Semitic Languages and Literatures*, 31 (1915), 169–214.

Orlinsky, H. M. "The Columnar Order of the Hexapla," *Jewish Quarterly Review*, 27 (1936–37); 137–149.

―――― "The Kings–Isaiah Recensions of the Hezekiah Story," *Jewish Quarterly Review*, 30 (1939–40), 33–49.

―――― *On the Present State of Proto-Septuagint Studies.* American Oriental Society Offprint Series, 13. New Haven, 1941.

―――― "The Septuagint — Its Use in Textual Criticism," *Biblical Archaeologist*, 9 (1946), 22–34.

―――― "Current Progress and Problems in Septuagint Research," *The Study of the Bible Today and Tomorrow*, ed. H. R. Willoughby. Chicago, 1947, pp. 141–161.

―――― "Qumran and the Present State of Old Testament Text Studies: The Septuagint Text," *JBL*, 78 (1959), 26–33.

―――― "The Textual Criticism of the Old Testament," *The Bible and the Ancient Near East*, ed. G. E. Wright, New York, 1961, pp. 113–132.

―――― *Max Leopold Margolis, Scholar and Teacher.* Philadelphia, 1962.

―――― "Studies in the Septuagint of the Book of Job, IV," *Hebrew Union College Annual*, 33 (1962), 119–151.

Pack, F. "Origen's Evaluation of Textual Variants in the Greek Bible," *Restoration Quarterly*, 4 (1960), 139–146.

Pavlovsky, V., and E. Vogt. "Die Jahre der Könige von Juda und Israel," *Biblica*, 45 (1964), 321–347.

Pelletier, André. *Lettre d'Aristée à Philocrate.* Paris, 1962.

Plein, Ina. "Erwägungen zur Überlieferung von 1 Reg. 11: 26–14: 20," *ZAW*, 78 (1966), 8–24.

Pretzl, O. "Septuaginta-Probleme im Buch der Richter," *Biblica*, 7 (1926), 233–269, 353–383.

von Rad, Gerhard. *Studies in Deuteronomy*, trans. David Stalker, Studies in Biblical Theology, No. 9. London, 1953.

Rahlfs, Alfred. *Studien zu den Königsbüchern.* Septuaginta Studien, I. Göttingen, 1904.

―――― *Lucians Rezension der Königsbücher.* Septuaginta Studien, III. Göttingen, 1911.

―――― *Verzeichnis der griechischen Handschriften des alten Testaments.* Berlin, 1914.

—— *Das Buch Ruth griechisch, als Probe einer kritischen Handausgabe der Septuaginta.* Stuttgart, 1922.

—— *Studien über den griechischen Text des Buches Ruth.* Berlin, 1922.

Redpath, H. A. "A Contribution towards Setting the Dates of the Translations of the Various Books of the Septuagint," *Journal of Theological Studies*, 7 (1906), 606–615.

Rehm, Martin. *Textkritische Untersuchungen zu den Parallelstellen der Samuel-Königsbücher und der Chronik.* Münster, 1937.

Reider, Joseph. *Prolegomena to a Greek–Hebrew and Hebrew–Greek Index to Aquila.* Philadelphia, 1916.

—— and Nigel Turner. *An Index to Aquila.* Supplements to *VT*, 12. Leiden, 1966.

Roberts, Bleddyn. *The Old Testament Text and Versions.* Cardiff, 1951.

—— "The Dead Sea Scrolls and the Old Testament Scriptures," *Bulletin of the John Rylands Library*, 36 (1953–54), 75–96.

—— "The Hebrew Bible since 1937," *Journal of Theological Studies*, 15 (1964), 253–264.

Rowley, H. H. "The Proto-Septuagint Question," *Jewish Quarterly Review*, 33 (1942–43), 497–499.

Rudolph, Wilhelm. "Zum Text der Königsbücher," *ZAW*, 63 (1951), 201–216.

—— *Chronikbücher.* Handbuch zum alten Testament. Tübingen, 1955.

Šanda, Albert. *Die Bücher der Könige.* Exegetisches Handbuch zum alten Testament. 2 vols. Münster, 1911.

Schedl, Claus. "Textkritische Bemerkungen zu den Synchronismen der Könige von Israel und Juda," *VT*, 12 (1962), 88–119.

Seeligmann, I. L. "Problemen en perspectieven in het modernne Septuaginta-onderzoek," *Jaarbericht Ex Oriente Lux*, 7 (1940), 359–390e.

—— *The Septuagint Version of Isaiah: A Discussion of its Problems.* Leiden, 1948.

—— "Indications of Editorial Alteration and Adaptation in the Massoretic Text and the Septuagint," *VT*, 11 (1961), 201–221.

Segert, Stanislav. "Semitische Marginalien I", *Archiv Orientalni*, 29 (1961), 80–95.

—— "Die Sprache der moabitischen Königsinschrift," *Archiv Orientalni*, 29 (1961), 197–267.

Sibinga, J. S. *The Old Testament Text of Justin Martyr*, I: *The Pentateuch.* Leiden, 1963.

Silberstein, Siegfried. "Über den Ursprung der im Codex Alexandrinus und Vaticanus des dritten Königsbuches der alexandrinischen Übersetzung überlieferten Textgestalt," *ZAW*, 13 (1893), 1–75; 14 (1894), 1–30.

Skehan, P. W. "A Fragment of the 'Song of Moses' (Deut. 32) from Qumran," *BASOR*, 136 (1954), 12–15.

———— "Exodus in the Samaritan Recension from Qumran," *JBL*, 74 (1955), 182–187.

———— "The Qumran Manuscripts and Textual Criticism," *Volume du Congrès Strasbourg 1956.* Supplements to *VT*, 4. Leiden, 1957, pp. 148–158.

———— "Qumran and the Present State of OT Studies: The Massoretic Text," *JBL*, 78 (1959), 21–25.

———— "The Biblical Scrolls from Qumran and the Text of the Old Testament," *Biblical Archaeologist*, 38 (1965), 87–100.

Soisalon-Soininen, Ilmari. *Die Textformen der Septuaginta-Übersetzung des Richterbuches.* Annales Academiae Scientiarum Fennicae, ser. B. tom. 72¹. Helsinki, 1951.

———— *Der Charakter der asterisierten Zusätze in der Septuaginta.* Annales Academiae Scientiarum Fennicae, ser. B, tom. 114. Helsinki, 1959.

———— *Die Infinitive in der Septuaginta.* Annales Academiae Scientiarum Fennicae, ser. B, tom. 132¹. Helsinki, 1965.

Sperber, Alexander. "The Problems of the LXX Recensions," *JBL*, 54 (1935), 73–92.

Stade, Bernhard. "Miscellen", *ZAW*, 4 (1884), 178.

———— and F. Schwally. *The Books of Kings.* The Sacred Books of the Old Testament. Leipzig, 1904.

Stendahl, Krister. *The School of St. Matthew.* Copenhagen, 1954.

Sundberg, Albert C., Jr. *The Old Testament of the Early Church.* Harvard Theological Studies, 20. Cambridge, Mass., 1964.

Swete, Henry B. *An Introduction to the Old Testament in Greek*, 2nd ed. Cambridge, Eng., 1914.

Talmon, Shemaryahu. "Aspects of the Textual Transmission of the Bible in the Light of Qumran Manuscripts," *Textus*, 4 (1964), 95–132.

Thackeray, H. St.J. "The Greek Translators of the Four Books of Kings," *Journal of Theological Studies*, 8 (1907), 262–278.

———— *A Grammar of the Old Testament in Greek.* Cambridge, Eng., 1909.

———— *The Septuagint and Jewish Worship: A Study in Origins*, 2nd ed. London, 1923.

———— *Some Aspects of the Greek Old Testament.* London, 1927.

———— *Josephus, the Man and the Historian.* New York, 1929.

Thiele, Edwin R. "The Chronology of the Kings of Judah and Israel," *Journal of Near Eastern Studies*, 3 (1944), 137–186.

———— *The Mysterious Numbers of the Hebrew Kings.* Chicago, 1951. 2nd rev. ed., Grand Rapids, 1965.

———— "A Comparison of the Chronological Data of Israel and Judah," *VT*, 4 (1954), 185–195.

———— "The Question of Coregencies among the Hebrew Kings," *A Stubborn Faith*, ed. E. C. Hobbs. Dallas, 1956, pp. 39–52.

—— "The Problem of Overlapping Reigns," *The Ministry*, 33 (1960), 33–35.

—— "The Synchronisms of the Hebrew Kings — A Re-evaluation: I," *Andrews University Seminary Studies*, 1 (1963), 128–138.

—— "The Synchronisms of the Hebrew Kings — A Re-evaluation: II," *Andrews University Seminary Studies*, 2 (1964), 120–136.

—— "Pekah to Hezekiah," *VT*, 16 (1966), 83–103.

—— "The Azariah and Hezekiah Synchronisms," *VT*, 16 (1966), 103–107.

Thornhill, Raymond. "The Greek Text of the Book of Ruth: A Grouping of Manuscripts according to Origen's Hexapla," *VT*, 3 (1953), 236–249.

—— "Six of Seven Nations: a Pointer to the Lucianic Text in the Heptateuch, with Special Reference to the Old Latin Version," *Journal of Theological Studies*, 10 (1959), 233–246.

Tournay, R. "Quelques relectures bibliques antisamaritaines," *RB*, 71 (1964), 504–536.

Vaccari, A. "In margine al commento di T. Mopsuesteno ai Salmi," *Miscellanea Giovanni Mercati*, I. Studi e Testi, 121. Rome, 1946, pp. 175–198.

—— "The Hesychian Recension of the Septuagint," *Biblica*, 46 (1965), 60–66.

Vannutelli, P. *Libri synoptici Veteris Testamenti seu librorum Regum et Chronicorum loci paralleli*. Rome, 1931.

Van Zyl, A. H. *The Moabites*. Leiden, 1960.

Vogt, Ernst. "Textus praemasoreticus ex Qumran," *Biblica*, 35 (1954), 263–266.

Wallis, Gerhard. "Die vierzig Jahre der achten Zeile der Mesa-Inschrift," *Zeitschrift des Deutschen Palästina–Vereins*, 81 (1965), 180–186.

Wellhausen, Julius. *Der Text der Bücher Samuelis*. Göttingen, 1871.

Wevers, John. "A Study in the Hebrew Variants in the Books of Kings," *ZAW*, 61 (1945–48), 43–76.

—— "Double Readings in the Books of Kings," *JBL*, 65 (1946), 307–310.

—— "Exegetical Principles Underlying the Septuagint Text of I Kings 2: 12–21: 43," *Oudtestamentische Studiën*, 8 (1950), 300–332.

—— "A Study in the Textual History of Codex Vaticanus in the Books of Kings," *ZAW*, 64 (1952), 178–189.

—— "Principles of Interpretation Guiding the Fourth Translator of the Book of the Kingdoms," *Catholic Biblical Quarterly*, 14 (1952), 40–56.

—— "Exegetical Principles Underlying the Greek Text of 2 Sam. 11: 2– I Kings 2: 11," *Catholic Biblical Quarterly*, 14 (1953), 30–45.

—— "Septuaginta-Forschungen I. Ausgaben und Texte," *Theologische Rundschau*, 22 (1954), 85–137.

—— "Septuaginta-Forschungen II. Die Septuaginta als Übersetzungsurkunde," *Theologische Rundschau*, 22 (1954), 171–190.

―――― "Proto-Septuagint Studies," *The Seed of Wisdom: Essays in Honour of T. J. Meek*, ed. W. S. McCullough. Toronto, 1964, pp. 58–77.

Whitley, C. F. "The Deuteronomic Presentation of the House of Omri," *VT*, 2 (1952), 137–152.

Yeivin, S. "Did the Kingdoms of Israel Have a Maritime Policy?" *Jewish Quarterly Review*, 50 (1959), 193–228.

Ziegler, Joseph. *Untersuchung zur Septuaginta des Buches Isaias.* Alttestamentliche Abhandlungen, XII, pt. 3. Münster, 1934.

―――― "Die Vorlage der Isaias-Septuaginta (LXX) und die erste Isaias-Rolle von Qumran (IQ Isa)" *JBL*, 78 (1959), 34–59.

Zuntz, Günther. "Der Antinoe Papyrus der Proverbia und das Prophetologion," *ZAW*, 68 (1956), 124–184.

―――― "Aristeas Studies II: Aristeas on the Translation of the Torah," *Journal of Semitic Studies*, 4 (1959), 109–126.

INDEX